W9-AXV-123

EDITORIAL DIRECTOR   Julie A. Schumacher
SENIOR EDITOR   Terry Ofner
PERMISSIONS   The Permissions Group, Glenview, IL

COVER ART THE VIETNAM WAR 1984 Kenneth Willhite

© 2001 Perfection Learning® Corporation
1000 North Second Avenue, P.O. Box 500
Logan, Iowa 51546-0500
Tel: 1-800-831-4190 • Fax: 1-712-644-2392
#78849 PB ISBN-13: 978-0-7891-5269-5 ISBN-10: 0-7891-5269-x

12 13 14 15 16 PP 12 11 10 09 08

TABLE OF CONTENTS

Features of the Student Book

Introducing the Theme

Preface The Preface introduces the student to the **Essential Question** of the book. This question, together with the cluster questions and thinking skills, will guide student reading throughout the anthology. Use the Preface to set a purpose for reading.

Prologue The Prologue combines a strong visual image with a thematically relevant song. The Prologue is designed to stimulate discussion and to set the tone for study of the anthology.

Creating Context The Creating Context section contains two essays, a timeline, a map, and a concept vocabulary list. These features will create a framework for learning and provide an opportunity to assess prior knowledge.

The Selections

Clusters The anthology is divided into four **clusters** of selections. The selections offer a mixture of fiction, nonfiction, and poetry.

Cluster Questions and Thinking Skills The selections in all but the last cluster are grouped around a **cluster question** and **thinking skill,** which are stated on the cluster opening page. Reading the selections in the cluster will help students answer the cluster question as well as exercise the thinking skill.

Responding to the Cluster Rather than interrupting the flow of reading with questions after every selection, *Literature & Thought* anthologies present discussion questions at the end of the cluster. Many of these discussion questions address more than one selection, giving students the opportunity to address a group of literary selections as a whole rather than as unconnected parts. These questions can also be used as prewriting prompts for the writing activity that follows the cluster questions.

Writing Activity All but the last cluster end with a writing activity that integrates the cluster question with the thinking skill.

The Final Cluster

The Final Cluster Having practiced several thinking skills and with a core of literature behind them, students should be able to approach the final cluster of selections independently.

Features of This Teacher Guide

Planning and Scheduling Options Use these strategies for planning a 4- to 6-week unit, a 1- to 2-week unit, or using the student book in conjunction with a novel.

What Do You Think? (anticipation guide) To assess your students' attitudes toward the Vietnam War, administer the anticipation guide on page 64.

Introducing the Theme These resources include strategies for teaching the Preface to set the **purpose** for reading; the Prologue for setting the **tone** of the theme study; and the Creating Context section for setting the framework, or **context**, of the unit.

Teaching the Critical Thinking Skill Each cluster in the teacher guide begins with a lesson plan and handout/overhead for modeling the cluster thinking skill.

Cluster Vocabulary Handouts and Tests Students can use the reproducible vocabulary sheet to reference challenging words in each selection and to prepare for the Cluster Vocabulary Tests.

Selection Resources Every selection in the student book is supported with the following teacher supports: selection summaries, reading hints, thinking skills, extension activities, discussion questions with suggested answers, and special focus sections that provide historical, literary, or bibliographic background on the selections.

Responding to the Cluster This resource page provides sample answers to the cluster questions.

Writing Activity Reproducible Sheet This graphic organizer integrates the writing activity and the cluster critical thinking skill.

Suggestions for Teaching the Final Cluster The final cluster provides an opportunity for students to demonstrate their mastery of the content knowledge and thinking skills. Look for the following features: a final cluster planning guide, cluster vocabulary, selection teacher support, handouts to help generate research, writing, and project ideas.

The Essay Prompt This open-book essay prompt is based on the *essential question* of the anthology. Use it as a culminating essay test. You may want to give extra credit to students who correctly use Concept Vocabulary words and words from the Cluster Vocabulary Sheets.

Sample Rubric Use or adapt the sample rubric prior to assigning, and while assessing, student writing.

Assessments

Discussing the Selection Use the discussion questions to assess student understanding of the selections.

Responding to the Cluster The questions on the Responding to the Cluster pages can be used as informal assessments of student understanding of the cluster content as well as the cluster thinking skill.

Cluster Vocabulary Tests These 10-point vocabulary tests assess student understanding of key vocabulary words.

Writing Activities Writing activities are ideal for assessing student understanding of the content and thinking skills of each cluster.

Essay Prompt Use the final essay prompt to assess student understanding of the *essential question* of the theme study.

Three Teaching Options for *Times of Change*

4- TO 6-WEEK UNIT

Three Teaching Options for *Times of Change*

1- TO 2-WEEK UNIT

Shorten the 4- to 6-week schedule by using one or more of the following strategies.
- Assign complete clusters to literary circles. Have each group share what they learn and/or teach the cluster to their classmates.
- Assign individual selections to groups. Have each group share what they learn and/or teach the selection to the entire class.
- Choose 8–10 significant selections for study by the entire class. The following list would provide a shortened exploration of the themes in *Times of Change.*

Title	Page	Title	Page
Jack Smith	23	A Piece of My Heart	71
On the Rainy River	33	Woodstock Nation	89
Hippies	53	The Summer of Vietnam	118
Farmer Nguyen	64	To Heal a Nation	129
The Massacre at My Lai	67		

USING *TIMES OF CHANGE* WITH RELATED LITERATURE

Before Reading the Related Work
- Introduce the theme and the purpose for reading using the Anticipation Guide (page 64 of this teacher guide). From *Times of Change* use the Preface (page 3), the Prologue (pages 4–5), and Creating Context (pages 9–14).
- Have students choose one or two selections and a poem to read from each cluster. Ask students to report on their selection and how it helped them answer the cluster question.

During Reading
- Ask students to relate the readings in *Times of Change* to themes, actions, or statements in the longer work.
- At strategic points, have students discuss how characters in the longer work would react to selections in the anthology.

After Reading
- Have students read the last cluster and respond to the cluster questions, drawing upon selections in the anthology as well as the longer work.
- Ask students to compare and contrast one or more selections in the anthology and a theme in the longer work.
- Allow students to choose a research topic from the options given in **Research, Writing, and Discussion Topics** (page 59) or **Assessment and Project Ideas** (page 60).

> ### Related Longer Works
>
> **The Things They Carried** by Tim O'Brien. [RL 9 IL 9 +] Paperback 4221501; Cover Craft 4221502.
>
> **In Country** by Bobbie Ann Mason. [RL 8 IL 9 +] Paperback 4020201; Cover Craft 4020202.
>
> **Park's Quest** by Katherine Paterson. [RL 5.5 IL 5–9] Paperback 4026301; Cover Craft 4026302.
>
> See page 63 of this guide for descriptions of these works and more related titles.

Teaching the Preface (page 3)

What Effect Did the Decade of the 60s Have on the United States?

The question above is the *essential question* that students will consider as they read *Times of Change: Vietnam and the 60s*. The literature, activities, and organization of the book will lead them to think critically about this question and, perhaps, to put the watershed decade of the 60s into perspective.

To help students shape their answers to the broad essential question, they will read and respond to four sections, or clusters. Each cluster addresses a specific question and thinking skill.

CLUSTER ONE What Were the Roots of the Conflict? **SUMMARIZING**
CLUSTER TWO What Was the War Experience? **ANALYZING**
CLUSTER THREE What Was Happening Back Home? **GENERALIZING**
CLUSTER FOUR Thinking on your own **SYNTHESIZING**

Notice that the final cluster asks students to think independently about their answer to the essential question—*What effect did the decade of the 60s have on the United States?*

Discussing the Preface Review the Preface with students. Point out the essential question as well as the cluster question addressed in each cluster. You may want to revisit the essential question after students complete each cluster. The last cluster addresses the essential question directly.

Teaching the Prologue (pages 4–5)

About the Text Bob Dylan was among the creators of a new genre of American music, the protest song. Released in 1964, "The Times They Are A-Changin'" became an anthem of the protest movement. Dylan, who released two albums of protest songs in the early 60s (*The Freewheelin' Bob Dylan* and *The Times They Are A-Changin'*), achieved the status of a prophet who expressed the consciousness of a new generation. Inducted into the Rock and Roll Hall of Fame in 1989, Dylan received a Grammy Award for Lifetime Achievement in 1991.

Discussing the Text
- How does the songwriter think people should respond to change? *Answers will vary. The song is a call to move with the times. Dylan challenges people to help build the new order or get out of the way.*
- What types of change might he be referring to? *Answers will vary. They might include the Civil Rights Movement, the War Against Poverty, student efforts to make college education more relevant, the generation gap, and growing criticism of the conflict in Vietnam.*
- What does this song say to you about change? the 60s? *Answers will vary.*
- Young people in the 60s interpreted this song as a call to build a better society. Comment on whether this song has the same meaning to your generation. *Answers will vary.*

Discussing the Image
- Why do you think this image was chosen to illustrate the idea "Times of Change"?
- What photograph or artwork would you choose to illustrate the subject of Vietnam and the 60s?

What Do You Know? (Anticipation Guide)

Use the reproducible anticipation guide on page 64 of this teacher guide to activate your students' prior knowledge of Vietnam and the 60s. Explain that their initial ideas might change as they explore the topic more deeply. You might want to have students complete the survey again at the end of their thematic study to see how their understanding has changed.

True or False (Write a *T* or *F* by each statement.)

_____ 1. Vietnam happened too long ago to really affect my life.

_____ 2. Antiwar protesters used only peaceful tactics.

_____ 3. The draft was fair.

_____ 4. Many Americans thought that antiwar protesters and draft evaders were traitors.

_____ 5. Only people who couldn't avoid the draft served in Vietnam.

_____ 6. Woodstock gave the hippies a chance to live their dreams of a better society.

_____ 7. Young Americans influenced the government through antiwar protests.

_____ 8. Americans generally trusted what the government said about Vietnam.

_____ 9. Public pressure forced the withdrawal of American troops from Vietnam.

_____ 10. Vietnam veterans were welcomed home as heroes.

_____ 11. The memory of Vietnam makes Americans reluctant to get involved in foreign wars.

_____ 12. At the end of the Vietnam conflict, America was a different nation.

Teaching the Creating Context Section (pages 9–14)

Use these Creating Context features to activate students' prior knowledge and build background about Vietnam and the 60s.

The Swinging Sixties by Donald R. Gallo and **A Dubious Crusade** by James A. Warren (pages 9–11)
Discussing the Essays
  * What characteristics of the 60s does Donald Gallo consider significant?
  * How does James A. Warren think the Vietnam War changed America?
  * What aspect of Vietnam or the 60s is of most interest to you?

Map of Southeast Asia in the 60s (page 11) Have students study the map of Southeast Asia. Use the following to open discussion on the map.
  * Why do you think Vietnam was often a target for foreign invasion?
  * Why do you think some Americans thought that stopping the spread of Communism into South Vietnam was key to keeping all of Southeast Asia free from the spread of Communism?

Vietnam and the 60s Timeline (pages 12–13) Students can use the timeline to get an encapsulated view of Vietnam and the 60s as well as to gain perspective on the selections in *Times of Change*. Use the following activities to engage students in the content of the timeline.
  * Prepare a classroom timeline to record the approximate time and place of the selections in *Times of Change: Vietnam and the 60s.*
  * Assign each student one event on the timeline and have them prepare a caption that summarizes the event and its importance.

Concept Vocabulary (page 14) The terms on this page are important to understanding Vietnam and the 60s. Use the following prompts to discuss the terms.
  * Discuss terms that may be new to students.
  * Have students add new concept words as they read the anthology.

CLUSTER ONE

Summarizing

I. Present this definition to students.

When **summarizing** you briefly state the main points of an event, discussion, or piece of writing.

II. Discuss with students how they already use the process of summarizing by sharing the situations below.

You summarize when you

- tell a friend about a movie you saw.
- answer the dinner table question "How was school today?"
- write an essay about your summer vacation.

Ask students to suggest other situations where summarizing would be used.

III. Explain to students that there were many conflicts during the 60s, not just the conflict in Vietnam. Use the following steps to show how students can summarize some of the other conflicts of the 60s.

A. Use the reproducible "Conflicts of the 60s" on the next page as an overhead transparency or blackline master.

B. Show students how one reader highlighted the references to conflicts in **Passage A**. Then note how the reader summarized the passage in her own words.

C. Ask students to complete **Passage B**, summarizing some of the other conflicts America experienced during the 60s. Answers will vary. Students can self- or peer-check their work using these criteria.

• Does the summary contain a topic sentence and the main point of each paragraph?

• Did the writer restate ideas in his or her own words?

D. Tell students to use summarizing as they read the other selections in the book.

Conflicts of the 60s

Cluster Question: What were the roots of the conflict?

Definition: When **summarizing** you briefly state the main points of an event, discussion, or piece of writing. A strong summary provides an overview of the subject, highlights important information, and restates the information in your own words.

Directions: The Vietnam War was the main conflict of 60s. There were, however, other conflicts during the period. Understanding these conflicts will give you a broader picture of the era and will give you insight into the roots, or causes, of the conflicts of the 60s.

The passages below are from "The Swinging Sixties," the essay in the Creating Context section of *Times of Change: Vietnam and the 60s*. Notice how one reader highlighted the conflicts she identified in **Passage A** and wrote a short summary of the passage based upon the highlighted sections. Follow the model and highlight the conflicts in **Passage B**. Write your summary in the space provided.

Passage A

More significantly, the **struggle for racial equality** begun in the late fifties continued with **demonstrations, voter registration drives, race riots, the murders of civil rights activists as well as innocent children,** and a march through Washington, D.C., **highlighted by Martin Luther King, Jr.'s "I have a dream" speech** and the singing of "We Shall Overcome."

—*from* "The Swinging Sixties," page 9

Summary: *The 60s were a decade of conflicts. One of the most important was the fight for racial equality.*

This fight included demonstrations, riots, and the murder of civil rights workers and leaders as well as

innocent children.

Passage B

Meanwhile, the race between the Soviets and the Americans for dominance in outer space continued, culminating on July 21, 1969, when U.S. astronauts Neil Armstrong and Edwin "Buzz" Aldrin stepped onto the surface of the moon.

At the same time, fighting escalated in Vietnam, with the horrors of war brought into everyone's homes on the television news each evening. As American casualties mounted, so did the protests against this war. "Make love, not war" became the slogan of the times, and people everywhere sang John Lennon's "Give Peace a Chance."

—*from* "The Swinging Sixties," page 9

Summary: _____

_____

_____

_____

_____

Cluster One Vocabulary

Watch for the following words as you read the selections in Cluster One. Record your own vocabulary words and definitions on the blank lines.

Ballad of the Green Berets   pages 16–17

ballad   song that tells a story
fate   destiny; doom

_____

_____

_____

_____

History   pages 18–19

allied   united; associated
occupied   took over; settled
pacified   tamed; calmed
prevailed   won; triumphed

_____

_____

_____

_____

The Gulf of Tonkin Resolution   pages 20–21

contrived   made-up; manipulated
enshrouded   veiled; concealed
fervor   enthusiasm; zeal
protracted   extended; drawn-out
provocation   incitement; cause

_____

_____

_____

_____

Jack Smith   pages 22–31

cynical   distrustful; skeptical
green   inexperienced; unseasoned
infantry   branch of the military composed of foot soldiers
infiltration   passing through enemy lines
milieu   environment; surroundings
retrospect   review; meditation on the past
romantic   lofty; unrealistic; idealized
sham   fake; pretense
succumb   submit; yield; give in

_____

_____

_____

_____

On the Rainy River   pages 32–47

acquiescence   agreement; acceptance
amortizing   paying off gradually
censure   blame; condemnation
consensus   agreement
fathom   comprehend; understand
imperative   command; necessity
naive   innocent; gullible
platitudes   clichés
reticence   silence; reserve
vigil   watch; guard

_____

_____

_____

_____

Ballad of the Green Berets by Sgt. Barry Sadler, pages 16–17   Song Lyrics

Summary

After Staff Sergeant Barry Sadler (1940–1989) earned his silver wings at jump school, he wanted to write a song about the airborne paratrooper service. His "Ballad of the Green Berets," written while recuperating from a leg wound received in Vietnam, was the number one hit single for 1966.

Reading Hint	Thinking Skill	Extension
As with all songs, it is best to hear them. If possible, play the song in class.	Ask students to *summarize* the image this ballad gives of American soldiers in Vietnam.	**The Ballad:** A ballad is a song or poem that presents a short dramatic narrative. Prompt students to watch for other narratives in this cluster that could be told in a ballad.

Vocabulary

ballad song that tells a story

fate destiny; doom

Discussing the Song Lyrics

1. How does the songwriter describe the Green Berets? (Recall) *These elite fighting men are "America's best." After passing a rigorous test, they bravely fight and die for freedom.*

2. Why do you think this ballad became a number one hit during the early years of the Vietnam conflict? (Analysis) *Answers will vary. Some may note that the ballad idealizes the heroism of American commandos and portrays the war as a noble battle for freedom.*

3. How well does this song fit your image of the soldiers who fought and died in Vietnam? (Analysis) *Answers will vary. Some students may feel that the song captures a spirit of genuine heroism. Others may think it applies only to professional soldiers and does not capture the experience of draftees who were not sure why they were fighting.*

Literary Focus: Tone

Tone is an author's attitude toward a subject. While this attitude can be expressed directly, it is often implied by descriptive words and characters' actions. These questions will help students analyze the tone of this ballad.

- Can you find any direct statements of Sadler's opinion about the Green Berets?
- What adjectives does Sadler use to describe these fighting men?
- Why do you think Sadler includes the "last request" mentioned in the fourth stanza?

History by Thuong Vuong-Riddick, pages 18–19   Poem

Summary

In a deadpan tone, this poem summarizes Vietnamese history as a series of conflicts culminating in the defeat of the American forces and the flight of many South Vietnamese.

Reading Hint	Thinking Skill	Extension
This poem's deadpan voice may confuse some. The impassive tone is deliberate—to convey the idea that Vietnam has always experienced war.	Summarize the main idea of this poem.	**Words that Show Emotion:** This poem was deliberately written with no words that show emotion. Have students list words that would convey emotions. What words might they insert in the poem to evoke emotions? What would such words do to the poem?

Vocabulary

allied united; associated

occupied took over; settled

pacified tamed; calmed

prevailed won; triumphed

Discussing the Poem

1. What one thing about Vietnamese history stands out in your mind after reading this poem? (Recall) *Answers will vary. Some students may remember specific details while others may have a general impression of ongoing conflict.*

2. What is the impact of repeating the word "killed"? (Analysis) *Answers will vary. The repetition emphasizes the destruction caused by the repeated invasions of Vietnam. The United States was just one of the countries involved in centuries of conflict on Vietnamese soil. While the nations involved vary, the results are the same.*

3. Why do you think the poet chooses to cover more than 1,000 years of history in a brief poem? (Analysis) *Answers will vary. From this perspective, Vietnamese history is a series of bloody wars for which the only resolution is exile. The focus is not on one person's tragedy, but on a nation's suffering.*

Literary Focus: Medium and Message

Ask students to compare "History" to the timeline on pages 12–13.

- What events are found in both works?
- What differences do you note between the timeline and the poem?
- How does the purpose of the timeline differ from the purpose of the poem?
- Why is the timeline considered a reference tool while the poem is a work of literature?

The Gulf of Tonkin Resolution by M. Hirsh Goldberg, pages 20–21 Article

Summary

After a reported attack on the destroyer *Maddox*, President Johnson asked Congress to authorize action to protect American forces and honor treaty obligations to South Vietnam. Goldberg outlines critics' suggestions that the Gulf of Tonkin incident was used as an excuse to deepen U.S. involvement in Vietnam.

Reading Hint	Thinking Skill	Extension
Students may be interested to know that this article was originally published in a book titled *The Book of Lies: History's Greatest Fakes, Frauds, Schemes, and Scams.*	Summarize the various points of view about the Gulf of Tonkin incident.	**Could It Happen Today?** Ask students to decide whether a story about an attack that never happened could be used to shape public opinion today. Have them develop questions or criteria for evaluating media coverage of acts of war.

Vocabulary

contrived made-up; manipulated

enshrouded veiled; concealed

fervor enthusiasm; zeal

protracted extended; drawn-out

provocation incitement; cause

Discussing the Article

1. What is the main point of this article? (Recall) *Author M. Hirsh Goldberg argues that the attack on the* Maddox—*which Johnson used to deepen our involvement in Vietnam—may never have happened.*

2. What do you think the author means by the phrase "bitter fighting both abroad and at home"? (Analysis) *Answers will vary. The author suggests that, while soldiers fought and died in Vietnam, public opinion in the United States became increasingly divided about the legitimacy of the war and the trustworthiness of military and government officials.*

Literary Focus: A Writer's Purpose

The form an article takes is influenced by the author's *purpose*. For example, in a news report, the reporter's purpose is to present the facts about current events. In a feature article, the writer strives to pique the reader's curiosity in a topic by presenting interesting or unusual information. In an editorial or opinion piece, the writer attempts to persuade the reader to take an action or agree with his or her point of view.

Use the following questions to prompt discussion about Goldberg's purpose.

- In which category of writing would you place "The Gulf of Tonkin Resolution"— news report, feature article, or opinion? Explain your choice.

- How might a news report about the the Gulf of Tonkin incident be different than an opinion piece?

- What do you think Sgt. Barry Sadler (the writer of the song "Ballad of the Green Berets") would say in response to Goldberg's article?

- Bias occurs when a writer favors one side in an argument by presenting only one point of view, or presenting more arguments against one side than another. In what way(s) might Goldberg's article be biased?

Jack Smith by Ron Steinman, pages 22–31

Oral History

Summary

In a first-person account, Jack Smith tells how, as a young American looking for adventure, he enlisted in the army. Early in the war, he is sent to Vietnam where nearly all the members of his unit are killed in an ambush. He finds it difficult to come to terms with defeat and the deaths of his comrades, but eventually regains faith in the human spirit.

Reading Hint	Thinking Skill	Extension
Tell students that this oral history is based on one of several interviews that Ron Steinman conducted with Vietnam veterans.	*Summarize* the reasons that Jack Smith considers himself a typical soldier.	**Flashbacks:** Have students imagine Jack Smith's reactions to the "Ballad of the Green Berets" before and after his experience in Vietnam.

Vocabulary

cynical distrustful; skeptical

green inexperienced; unseasoned

infantry branch of the military composed of foot soldiers

infiltration passing through enemy lines

milieu environment; surroundings

retrospect review; meditation on the past

romantic lofty; unrealistic; idealized

sham fake; pretense

succumb submit; yield; give in

Discussing the Oral History

1. Why does Jack Smith consider himself a typical enlistee? (Recall) *Like many 19-year-olds at the time, he joined the army to grow up and have some adventure before college.*

2. How was Jack Smith affected by his experiences in Vietnam? (Analysis) *Answers will vary. At first, he became cynical and contemptuous of human weakness. Then he discovered a renewed appreciation for life and the endurance of the human spirit.*

3. How would you respond to Jack Smith's question: "What . . . was the point . . ."? (Analysis) *Answers will vary. Students will have different opinions about whether the war was necessary and what justifies sending American soldiers into combat on foreign soil.*

Literary Focus: Oral History

An *oral history* is a first-person account based on interviews. Some oral historians translate their subjects' words from spoken to written language. In the process, they edit out verbal tics (such as repeated *uhs* or *ums*) and note gestures where appropriate (*draws index finger across throat*).

Discuss these questions with students.

- What made Jack Smith's account of combat convincing or unconvincing to you?
- What makes this oral history different from a short story or article about Vietnam?
- Agree or disagree: Oral histories are first-person testimony. Therefore, they are always reliable.
- Why do you think Ron Steinman believed it was important to collect oral histories of the war in Vietnam?

Discussing the Images

- This oral history is illustrated with a drawing and a photograph. Explain which you think is more effective.
- Use information from Jack Smith's description of combat to write a caption for one of the illustrations.

On the Rainy River   by Tim O'Brien, pages 32–47   Short Story

Summary
A would-be draft dodger flees to the Canadian border. There he meets an older man who, through quiet patience, helps the young man make a difficult choice.

Reading Hint	Thinking Skill	Extension
Tell students that this selection is a semifictionalized account of the author's own experience.	*Summarize* the narrator's attitude toward the conflict in Vietnam.	**To Be a Hero:** This story hinges on the idea of heroism. Have students discuss the following proposition: The narrator was showing true heroism by returning to Minnesota.

Vocabulary

acquiescence agreement; acceptance

amortizing paying off gradually

censure blame; condemnation

consensus agreement

fathom comprehend; understand

imperative command; necessity

naive innocent; gullible

platitudes clichés

reticence silence; reserve

vigil watch; guard

Discussing the Short Story

1. Why does the speaker object to the conflict in Vietnam? (Recall) *He thinks confusion over the war make it impossible to determine the rightness of American involvement.*
2. Describe the speaker's conflict over serving in Vietnam. (Analysis) *Answers will vary. The speaker is torn between his belief that the war is wrong and his fear of disappointing those who are important to him.*
3. What does the Rainy River represent to the speaker? (Analysis) *Answers will vary. He says the river "for me separated one life from another." Crossing to Canada would honor his conscience; remaining in the U.S. would force him to fight for a cause he doesn't believe in.*
4. Why do you think the speaker says that Elroy Berdahl saved his life? (Analysis) *Answers will vary. The man didn't ask questions or probe; he just let the speaker make his decision.*

Special Focus: Conscientious Objectors

Conscientious objectors are individuals who are exempted from military duty because their religious beliefs forbid participation in warfare. Use the following questions to discuss this issue.
- Do you think it is fair for some people to get out of serving in the military for religious reasons? Why or why not?
- In your opinion, should conscientious objectors be made to serve in other ways besides combat?

About the Author: Tim O'Brien

O'Brien served in the army from 1968–1970 and earned a Purple Heart in Vietnam.

In a 1994 *New York Times* essay, he wrote, "When the draft notice arrived after graduation . . . I thought about Canada. I thought about jail. But in the end, I could not bear the prospect of rejection: by my family, my friends, my country, my hometown." The struggle between his conscience and his fear of rejection was, he said, "worse than being in the war."

Other titles by Tim O'Brien
- *If I Die in a Combat Zone, Box Me Up and Ship Me Home,* based on his army service
- *Going After Cacciato,* winner of the National Book Award, about a soldier who decides to run away from the war
- *The Things They Carried,* a collection of interconnected stories
- *In the Lake of the Woods,* with a hero who participated in the My Lai massacre

What Were the Roots of the Conflict?

Thinking Skill: SUMMARIZING

1. What does the poem "History" tell you about Vietnam's past? *Answers will vary. Most students will probably comment on the continuous conflict on Vietnam soil.*

2. The main characters (or speakers) in this cluster express definite opinions about the conflict in Vietnam. Using a chart such as the one below, **summarize** these opinions.

Individual	Summary Sentence
Speaker of "Ballad of the Green Berets"	*American soldiers in Vietnam bravely fought and died for freedom.*
Speaker of "History"	*The Vietnam War was one of a series of seemingly endless bloody conflicts.*
Author of "Gulf of Tonkin Resolution . . ."	*Congress was manipulated into approving increased American military involvement in Vietnam.*
Jack Smith	*Nothing justifies American losses in Vietnam.*
Narrator of "On the Rainy River"	*The war is hateful because American had no compelling reason to fight in Vietnam.*

3. Compare Jack Smith's attitude toward the war at the beginning with his attitude at the conclusion of his story. *Answers will vary. At first, he is naive. He doesn't expect to see combat and isn't sure why the U.S. is in Vietnam. Nonetheless, he forms intense relationships with his buddies and is willing to fight to protect them. He, of course, is grief-stricken and bitter at the loss of his companions. Looking back, he has recovered from his initial bitterness but still wonders "what . . . was the point . . . ?"*

4. Near the end of the short story "On the Rainy River," Tim O'Brien calls himself a coward. Do you agree with his assessment? Why or why not? *Answers will vary. Some will agree that he didn't have the courage to live up to his own convictions. Others may disagree, noting that the narrator wrote the account as a way to thank Elroy Berdahl for "saving his life." The narrator must feel that his return to the U.S. and to fight in a war that he didn't believe in took courage as well.*

5. How did the United States government justify its military involvement in Vietnam? *Answers will vary. Supporters of the domino theory argued that Vietnam must remain free to keep its neighbors free. Others felt that the U.S. must respond to the alleged attack on the* USS Maddox.

Writing Activity: A Poetic Summary

The handout on page 19 provides a graphic organizer to help students with the writing activity. You may also wish to use the Writing Activity Handout as an assessment. See also page 62 for a sample rubric to use with student projects.

Writing Activity: A Poetic Summary

Definition: When **summarizing** you briefly state the main points of an event, discussion, or piece of writing.

Directions: The poem "History" summarizes centuries of conflict in thirty-one lines. Using the information in this cluster and what you already know, write a poem that summarizes some aspect of the war in Vietnam.

Poets use different techniques to summarize, or compress, themes and feelings into a few well-chosen words. For example, the poet of "History" *catalogs*, or lists, a series of wars fought in Vietnam. The poet unifies the poem by following chronological order and repeating the word *killed*.

Another approach is to build a poem around a single image. By focusing on a single event—say the death of a soldier—the poet lets the details stand for a larger meaning: the cruelty of war or the courage and sacrifice of soldiers.

Use one of the above techniques (or another approach of your own) to compose your poem. You might use the chart below to help generate ideas. There is no "right" way to compose a poem. Use this chart as a place to "think on paper." Don't feel that you have to fill in every blank. For example, you might get an idea for a poem by listing several key words. Once you have a poem started, come back to your chart only if you are stuck.

Topic or Theme _____

_____

_____

Main Image or Event _____

_____

_____

Will you use a list or catalog? If so, what events or objects will you list? _____

_____

_____

_____

Key Words _____

_____

_____

_____

Other_____

_____

_____

Use the best images, words, lists, topics in your poem. Remember, a strong poem

- places emphasis on language as well as the topic.
- may employ rhythm and/or rhyme.
- may use figurative language (simile, metaphor, and personification).

Cluster One Vocabulary Test

Pages 16–47

Choose the meaning of the bold word in each passage.

1. Her Green Beret has met his **fate.**
   (*"Ballad of the Green Berets," p. 16*)

   Ⓐ goal   Ⓒ comrades
   Ⓑ accident   Ⓓ destiny

2. . . .the Chinese . . . called Vietnam, Annam, which means / "The **Pacified** South."
   (*"History," p. 18*)

   Ⓐ beautiful   Ⓒ calmed
   Ⓑ friendly   Ⓓ fertile

3. Many now say [the Gulf of Tonkin] episode was **contrived** . . .
   (*"The Gulf of Tonkin Resolution," p. 21*)

   Ⓐ convincing   Ⓒ decisive
   Ⓑ manipulated   Ⓓ unplanned

4. . . . 55,000 Americans lost their lives in one of the most **protracted** wars the United States has ever waged.
   (*"The Gulf of Tonkin Resolution," p. 21*)

   Ⓐ extended   Ⓒ expensive
   Ⓑ unpopular   Ⓓ misguided

5. . . . I had a **romantic** notion about the army and war and that sort of thing.
   (*"Jack Smith," p. 23*)

   Ⓐ unrealistic   Ⓒ disillusioned
   Ⓑ cynical   Ⓓ green

6. You haven't yet acquired adult friends, an adult job, an adult **milieu** in which you move. (*"Jack Smith," p. 31*)

   Ⓐ home   Ⓒ responsibility
   Ⓑ environment   Ⓓ dream

7. I was twenty-one years old. Young, yes, and politically **naive** . . .
   (*"On the Rainy River," p. 33*)

   Ⓐ knowledgeable Ⓒ suspicious
   Ⓑ innocent   Ⓓ smart

8. . . . when a nation goes to war it must have reasonable confidence in the justice and **imperative** of its cause.
   (*"On the Rainy River," p. 34*)

   Ⓐ reasonableness Ⓒ arguability
   Ⓑ efficiency   Ⓓ necessity

9. . . . I detested their blind, thoughtless, automatic **acquiescence** . . .
   (*"On the Rainy River," p. 36*)

   Ⓐ concern   Ⓒ acceptance
   Ⓑ patriotism   Ⓓ platitudes

10. I feared ridicule and **censure.**
    (*"On the Rainy River," p. 36*)

    Ⓐ blame   Ⓒ combat
    Ⓑ laughter   Ⓓ silence

CLUSTER TWO

Analyzing

I. Present this definition to students.

When you **analyze** you break down a topic or subject into parts so that it is easier to understand.

II. Discuss with students how they already use analyzing by sharing the situations below.

You use analyzing when you

- study the moves of an outstanding athlete.
- learn the rules of a new game.
- learn how to use new software.

Have students suggest other situations where analyzing would be used.

III. Explain to students that they will be analyzing the selections in Cluster Two to find out what it was like to experience the war.

A. Use the reproducible "Analyzing the War" on the next page as an overhead transparency or blackline master.

B. Show how one reader analyzed **Passage A.**

C. Have students analyze **Passage B** using **Passage A** as a model. If necessary, point out the following details. With students, help them find other details that help describe the war experience.

- "we were a little apprehensive" points out the vulnerability of those in combat situations.
- "I hope they (meaning our commanding officers) know what they are doing." This passage shows that soldiers look to their officers for guidance and direction.

Analyzing the War

Cluster Question: What Was the War Experience?

Definition: With **analysis** you break down a topic or subject into parts so that it is easier to understand.

Directions: Notice how one reader analyzed **Passage A** and highlighted passages that reveal what life is like for a soldier. Notice also how the reader explained the highlighted text. Analyze **Passage B** by underlining details that provide insight into the war experience. Then write a short explanation of each detail.

Details

Passage A

I signed up for the Special Forces because **I had a romantic notion about the army and war** and that sort of thing. I wanted to have an adventure for a few years. Through various twists and turns, and the military bureaucracy, I ended up in the infantry. **We spent most of our time cleaning our rifles,** going on war maneuvers, war games, getting into trouble, very **boring barracks duty.** Then all of a sudden, one day we were told that all the short-timers were going to be let out of the army. People who had longer time to serve would be merged with an experimental unit called the 11th Air Assault. . . . Then one day in July we listened to Lyndon Johnson give a speech when he announced that he was sending us, the 1st Cavalry Division over to Vietnam and that he was, in effect, declaring war on North Vietnam without really declaring war on North Vietnam. **That's when it hit us that we were going into combat.**

—*from* "Jack Smith," pages 23–24

Many people joined the army for lack of anything better to do and for adventure.

Army life could be boring and tedious.

A soldier's life can be unpredictable.

Details

Passage B

The next day we walked to Landing Zone Albany for what we thought was extraction, being lifted out by helicopter. We were out for a Sunday stroll in the woods. We were strolling along, and we were a little apprehensive because we knew there had been this huge battle. We'd seen the bodies. Leaving the landing zone, you walk on bodies a hundred feet outside the dry creek bed and the foxholes. We knew there were a lot of enemy units around and some of us were a little apprehensive about walking in such a casual fashion. But we did, and a number of us remarked on it. "Shouldn't we have guards out?" And, "There are probably bad guys around here. I hope we don't get ambushed. I hope they (meaning our commanding officers) know what they are doing."

—*from* "Jack Smith," page 26

Cluster Two Vocabulary

Watch for the following words as you read the selections in Cluster Two. Record your own vocabulary words and definitions on the blank lines.

I-Feel-Like-I'm-Fixin'-To-Die Rag
pages 50–51

au French word meaning "with"
pearly gates gates of heaven
rag a song in ragtime, with a snappy melody and regularly accented accompaniment

_____

_____

Hippies pages 52–55

communal shared; mutual
conventional traditional; accepted
ethos ethic; set of values
illusion dream; fantasy; delusion
phenomenon extraordinary person or event
scarcity want; poverty
trite commonplace; ordinary; clichéd

_____

_____

Village pages 56–63

barrio Spanish term for neighborhood
discord conflict; disharmony
furtively secretly; stealthily; covertly
intuitive instinctive; not based on reason
marrow core; basic nature
pyre combustible heap; pile of material to be burned
queuing filing; lining up
tumult turmoil; agitation
undulant rising and falling; wave-like

_____

_____

Farmer Nguyen pages 64–65

hamlet small village
Round Eyes slang term for Americans

_____

_____

The Massacre at My Lai pages 66–68

atrocity outrage; monstrous act
condemn blame; denounce
confronted approached; spoke with
flailing moving; thrashing
massacre slaughter; extermination
premeditated planned; thought-out
scenarios possible sequences of events

_____

_____

A Nun in Hinh Hoa page 69

mocking laughing at; defying

_____

_____

A Piece of My Heart pages 70–77

complacent self-satisfied; unconcerned
disoriented confused; mixed-up
innocuous harmless; inoffensive
invincible unconquerable; not subject to harm
loathing hatred; hostility; antipathy
maternal motherly
preconception prejudgment; prejudice
reluctantly unwillingly; hesitantly
traumatic disturbing; upsetting; shocking
vulnerable exposed; unprotected

_____

_____

I-Feel-Like-I'm-Fixin'-To-Die Rag by Joe McDonald, pages 50–51   Song Lyrics

Summary

One of many songs the author wrote to protest the Vietnam War, this rag criticizes "the politicians and leaders of the U.S. military and . . . the industry that makes its money from war."

Reading Hint	Thinking Skill	Extension
Some students may be offended by the tone of this song. It is included here for historical accuracy.	Have students identify lines in which they find a contrast between what is said and what is meant.	**Black Humor:** Death in battle is usually considered a serious topic. Ask students if they think the use of black humor is appropriate for such a topic.

Vocabulary

au French word meaning "with"

pearly gates gates of heaven

rag a song in ragtime, with a snappy melody and regularly accented accompaniment

Discussing the Song Lyrics

1. Identify one thing that this song protests. (Recall) *Answers might include American involvement in Vietnam, the military and business establishments, the draft, and uncritical patriotism.*

2. Who does the author blame for the Vietnam war? (Analysis) *Answers will vary. He blames the war on those who believe that destruction can achieve peace and on those who stand to gain monetarily from the war.*

3. Do you think it is appropriate to make light of dying in combat? (Analysis) *Answers will vary. Some may object to a light tone because it dishonors those that have died. Others may feel that it is appropriate to use a light tone in a song that protests war.*

Literary Focus: GI Humor

"Country" Joe McDonald recalls that he wrote this song in 1965, as students were demonstrating against the war. "The song attempts to address the horror of going to war with a dark sarcastic form of humor called 'GI humor,' " he explains in an essay on his Web site. "GI humor is a way people have of complaining about their situation so it will not get them in trouble and keep them from going insane in an insane environment: war."

Share the author's comments about GI humor with students. Then work with them to
- find examples of sarcasm in the lyrics.
- describe how the author uses GI humor to make a serious point.

Discussing the Cluster Opener

The image on page 49 of is one of the most haunting photographs of the Vietnam War. Taken on June 8, 1972, by an AP photographer, the photo features a nine-year-old girl who was badly scorched by napalm. The photographer and a British correspondent took the girl to a hospital in Saigon where an international team of doctors saved her life after 17 operations. Today she lives in Ontario, Canada, with her husband and two sons. Despite living with constant pain, she leads an active life as a volunteer goodwill ambassador for a United Nations Organization and the head of a foundation for child victims of war.

Hippies by Alex Forman, pages 52–55

Memoir

Summary

In 1967, the author thought that communal living in Haight-Ashbury was the beginning of a new society. As abundance turned to scarcity, he realized that the promise of a new society was an illusion.

Reading Hint	Thinking Skill	Extension
Before students read, discuss their ideas of a utopia, or perfect world.	Contrast the author's experience of Haight-Ashbury at the beginning and the end of 1967.	**The Hippie Legacy:** Forman seems to suggest that the hippie culture ended as soon as it started. But hippie values impacted mainstream culture for better and for worse. List with students some of the legacies of the hippie era. For example, tie-dyed clothing, idealism, relaxed lifestyle.

Vocabulary

communal shared; mutual

conventional traditional; accepted

ethos ethic; set of values

illusion dream; fantasy; delusion

phenomenon extraordinary person or event

scarcity want; poverty

trite commonplace; ordinary; clichéd

Discussing the Memoir

1. Describe the author's first reaction to Haight-Ashbury. (Recall) *Initially, Haight-Ashbury seems like a communal "paradise" in which abundance makes it possible for people to enjoy life and create an alternative society.*

2. Contrast the hippies' values with those of mainstream society. (Analysis) *Answers will vary. The hippies valued freedom, sharing, enjoying life, experiencing nature, and peace. They wanted to avoid being trapped by conventional morality and the desire to accumulate possessions.*

3. How did the author learn about scarcity? (Analysis) *Answers will vary. He describes an incident in which three poor women took clothes he was giving away, planning to sell them. The hippies assumed people would take only what they needed to wear; the women saw an opportunity to get some desperately needed income.*

4. Why does the author call the counterculture an "illusion"? (Analysis) *Answers will vary. Abundance created a false impression that food, clothing, and cheap lodging would always be plentiful. In addition, the conflict in Vietnam continued.*

Literary Focus: Memoir

An autobiography is the story of a person's life as told by that person. A *memoir* is also a first-person account, but the narrator tends to focus on people he has known or historical events she has experienced. A memoir is not just one person's story; it can describe an entire period in history from one person's perspective.

Discuss these questions with students.

- What did you learn about the counterculture from this memoir?
- Why do you think the author includes the story about the free store?
- How does he relate his memories to the conflict in Vietnam?

Village   by Estela Portillo, pages 56–63

Short Story

Summary

Rico, an Hispanic soldier, observes a Vietnamese village and is reminded of the neighborhood where he grew up. When his sergeant orders the destruction of the village, Rico shoots him in the arm to stop the action. Rico will be court-martialed and imprisoned, but feels free knowing that he saved innocent people.

Reading Hint	Thinking Skill	Extension
Have students watch for these key words in the story: *memory, erased,* and *freedom.*	*Analyze* the internal conflict Rico experiences as the platoon prepares to destroy the village.	**Closing Arguments:** Ask students to choose whether they would defend or prosecute Rico at his court-martial. Then have them write a brief speech summarizing the reasons they believe Rico should be punished or acquitted.

Vocabulary

barrio Spanish term for neighborhood

discord conflict; disharmony

furtively secretly; stealthily; covertly

intuitive instinctive; not based on reason

marrow core; basic nature

pyre combustible heap; pile of material to be burned

queuing filing; lining up

tumult turmoil; agitation

undulant rising and falling; wave-like

Discussing the Short Story

1. What conflict does Rico experience at the beginning of the story? (Recall) *His superiors consider the village of Mai Cao a threat, but he sees only peaceful people who remind him of those at home.*

2. Why does Rico think that following orders would be "the easy thing to do"? (Analysis) *Answers will vary. Following orders would make the sergeant, not Rico, responsible for the villagers' deaths. Rico could remain one of the guys instead of having to face accusations of cowardice.*

3. Do you think Rico did the right thing? (Analysis) *Answers will vary. Most will probably say yes, citing Rico's feeling of freedom at the end of the story. Some may say that it is the duty of a soldier to follow orders, otherwise, there will be chaos.*

4. How do you think Rico will explain his actions at his court-martial? (Analysis) *Answers will vary. He will be tried for not doing his duty as a soldier, but he chose to be a human being first and a soldier second. Had he followed orders without question, innocent people would have died.*

Literary Focus: Conflict

When Rico compares a Vietnamese village to his barrio, he finds "people all the same everywhere." This comparison creates *conflict* when his platoon is ordered to destroy the village.

   The following questions will help students explore *conflict* in this story.

- What creates the conflict between the villagers and the American soldiers? *Orders have come down to destroy the village to prevent it from becoming an enemy base.*

- Describe the conflict between Rico's mind and heart. *Rico knows that guerrillas often disguise themselves as Vietnamese civilians, but he believes that the villagers are noncombatants.*

- How does Rico's action bring him into conflict with his superiors? his friend Harry? *Rico is arrested and will face court-martial. His sergeant ignores him. Harry tells Rico he will never be a soldier.*

- How do you think the conflict will be resolved? *Answers will vary. Rico will probably be confined after his court-martial.*

Farmer Nguyen by W. D. Ehrhart, pages 64–65   Poem

Summary
A Vietnam veteran describes how a farmer is victimized by soldiers on both sides of the conflict.

Reading Hint	Thinking Skill	Extension
Tell students that this poem is written by a Vietnam veteran.	*Analyze* the way both sides treated the farmer.	**A Different Perspective:** Ask students to rewrite the poem from the farmer's perspective.

Vocabulary
hamlet small village

Round Eyes slang term for Americans

Discussing the Poem

1. What happens to Farmer Nguyen when the soldiers come? (Recall) *He is twice accused of cooperating with the other side and beaten. The Americans beat and imprison him; the Vietcong confiscate supplies.*

2. How much choice did the farmer have about giving rice to the Vietcong? (Analysis) *Answers will vary. The speaker says that the Vietcong "took more rice," suggesting that in neither case did the farmer give it voluntarily.*

3. Why do you think the poet focused on one simple farmer? (Analysis) *Answers will vary. The poem shows the impact of the war on Vietnamese civilians. As opposing armies repeatedly enter and leave his village, the farmer's person and property are put at risk and his personal opinions seem irrelevant. The author also suggests that both sides treated the civilian population unfairly, even though the war was supposedly fought on its behalf.*

Literary Focus: Purpose for Writing
Authors have many purposes for writing, ranging from expressing feelings to creating images to making a point. Use the following to trigger a discussion.

- Why do you think W.D. Ehrhart wrote this poem?
- Who is the speaker in the poem?
- Why does he address the poem to Farmer Nguyen?

Discussing the Image

- Why do you think the image on page 65 was chosen to illustrate this poem?
- Write a caption that effectively expresses the meaning of both the poem and the photograph.

The Massacre at My Lai   by Hugh Thompson, pages 66–68   Essay

Summary

When Warrant Officer Hugh Thompson discovered the U.S. Army's Charlie Company killing unarmed civilians, he put his chopper into the line of fire to protect the villagers. He and his crew received the Soldier's Medal for saving at least 10 noncombatants from being murdered.

Reading Hint	Thinking Skill	Extension
The name of the village is pronounced Me-Lie.	In this essay, Hugh Thompson is called a hero; in "Village" Rico is imprisoned. *Analyze the reasons for the different treatments.*	**Citation for Bravery:** Ask students to draft wording for a citation commending the bravery of Hugh Thompson and his crew.

Vocabulary

atrocity outrage; monstrous act

condemn blame; denounce

confronted approached; spoke with

flailing moving; thrashing

massacre slaughter; extermination

premeditated planned; thought-out

scenarios possible sequences of events

Discussing the Essay

1. How does Thompson save the people hiding in the bunker? (Recall) *He lands his chopper between the soldiers and the villagers and orders his crew to return fire if the soldiers shoot at the villagers.*

2. What evidence does the author give to support his claim that "My Lai . . . was pure, premeditated murder"? (Analysis) *Thompson notes that he saw only one person who might be an enemy soldier in the village. He describes how an injured girl is shot by a captain, concludes that villagers were led into a ditch and executed, and intervenes to protect villagers hiding in a bunker.*

3. Thompson's actions at My Lai are now being used to teach battlefield ethics. Why do you think this is so? (Analysis) *Answers will vary. Students may note that Thompson, though outnumbered, did his best to stop the murder of innocent people. He saved 10 civilians at the risk of his own life. When he received the Soldier's Medal, Thompson was cited for "heroism [that] exemplifies the highest standards of personal courage and ethical conduct."*

4. How do you think news of the My Lai massacre affected American public opinion? (Analysis) *Answers will vary. When the massacre became public knowledge in 1969, horror—along with outrage at mounting American casualties—began to turn public opinion against the war.*

Literary Focus: Forgotten Hero

Hugh C. Thompson, Jr. (1943–) was awarded the Soldier's Medal in 1998 for heroism and voluntarily risking his life in conditions other than combat against the enemy. His life is chronicled in *The Forgotten Hero of My Lai: The Hugh Thompson Story,* by Trent Angers (Arcadian House, 1999). Use these details to help students appreciate why he is called the "Forgotten Hero."

• When Thompson reported the atrocity, headquarters ordered a stop to the killing. General W. R. Peers, who led the investigation, noted that Thompson and his crew were the only ones who tried to protect the villagers.

• It took 30 years for Thompson's heroism to be recognized. Politicians and the Pentagon tried to suppress the story. But Thompson insisted that the award, which was approved in 1996, be presented publicly, not just to him, but to his crew as well.

A Nun in Ninh Hoa by Jan Berry, page 69   Poem

Summary

A young American soldier is shaken when he witnesses the self-immolation of a Buddhist nun.

Reading Hint	Thinking Skill	Extension
Students may be shocked by the description of self-immolation in this poem. Assure them that such events actually happened.	Do you think the nun's action produced the desired end? Why or why not?	**Forms of Protest:** During the 1960s more than 100 monks and nuns immolated themselves (burned themselves alive) as a nonviolent protest against religious persecution and the war. Have students keep a log of the various ways people protested the war in Vietnam. Which forms seemed most effective?

Vocabulary

mocking laughing at; defying

Discussing the Poem

1. What was Jimmy doing when he saw this shocking sight? (Recall) *He was out riding on a fuel truck convoy.*

2. What was the nun's demeanor as she died? (Recall) *She was calm and smiling, perhaps mockingly.*

3. Describe Jimmy Sharpe's reaction to seeing a nun burn herself to death. (Recall) *The "nightmare" makes him wonder "How'd we get in this crazy place?"*

4. Why do you think Jimmy Sharpe reacts as he does to the nun's death? (Analysis) *Answers will vary. Nothing in his background prepares him to understand what he has witnessed. From his perspective, the act seems inexplicable and "crazy." His sense of the cultural differences between the U.S. and Vietnam makes him question whether Americans belong in Vietnam.*

Special Focus: Self-Immolation

Students may have these questions about the self-immolation.

- Why did the nun burn herself to death? *In Buddhist tradition, self-immolation is considered a nonviolent form of protest. During the war, more than 100 Buddhists monks and nuns immolated themselves as a protest against the suffering caused by the war.*

- How did Americans react to these deaths? *Some Americans saw the deaths as an attempt to manipulate public opinion. Others considered the monks and nuns martyrs for peace.*

Ask students the following.

- Do you think the nun's protest did any good?

- What were other ways of protesting the war?

A Piece of My Heart by Anne Simon Auger, pages 70–77   Oral History

Summary

As she begins her service in Vietnam, the author is an inexperienced yet eager nurse who feels "invincible." As she encounters the horrors of combat, however, she learns to build up walls between herself and the wounded GIs—walls that persist long after the war.

Reading Hint	Thinking Skill	Extension
As students read, have them watch for the contrast between feelings of invincibility and vulnerability.	*Analyze* the reasons Auger has difficulty fitting in when she came back home.	**Women in Vietnam:** Ask students to identify what was expected of Auger when she served in Vietnam. Discuss whether they think these expectations are appropriate for women in the armed forces.

Vocabulary

complacent self-satisfied; unconcerned

disoriented confused; mixed-up

innocuous harmless; inoffensive

invincible unconquerable; not subject to harm

loathing hatred; hostility; antipathy

maternal motherly

preconception prejudgment; prejudice

reluctantly unwillingly; hesitantly

traumatic disturbing; upsetting; shocking

vulnerable exposed; unprotected

Discussing the Oral History

1. What attitude does the author have toward going to Vietnam? (Recall) *She feels "excited" and ready for new experiences.*

2. Describe a lesson that the author learns during her service in Vietnam. (Analysis) *Answers will vary. Auger now feels that the walls she put up to distance herself from her patients' suffering may have prevented her from understanding and responding to their trauma. On the Vietnamese ward, she learns that "nobody is safe from war." She confronts her capacity to hate, recognizes her vulnerability, learns to rely on herself instead of waiting to be taken care of, and discovers empathy for the suffering.*

3. Why does the author feel disoriented when she returns home? (Analysis) *Answers will vary. After her "traumatic" experiences, she feels jumpy and out of touch with everyday life and the "complacent" people back home. She finds it difficult to talk about her time in Vietnam, believing that most people wanted to pretend that she'd never been away.*

Special Focus: The Theme of Walls

One of the central themes of this essay is the mental wall that Auger built to protect herself from the loss and suffering of the war. With students, explore the concept of walls. As students continue through the anthology, have them watch for other images or references to walls. Use the following concepts to prompt further thinking and discussion.

- Walls separate people.
- Walls isolate people.
- Walls provide privacy.
- Walls give protection.
- Walls separate countries, as with the Great Wall of China or the Berlin Wall.
- What else can serve as a wall? a fence? silence?

What Was the War Experience?

Thinking Skill: ANALYZING

1. **Tone** is a writer's attitude toward the subject he or she is writing about. For example, a writer might take a playful, somber, or sarcastic attitude toward a topic. **Analyze** the tone of "I-Feel-Like-I'm-Fixin'-To-Die Rag" and "The Ballad of the Green Berets." *Answers will vary. Both authors write with conviction and both try to persuade others to share their point of view. However, their ideas about the nobility and purpose of the war differ. "Country" Joe McDonald's antiwar song satirizes the generals who "got . . . in a terrible jam," the suppliers who make money from "war au-go-go," and parents who send their sons to battle out of blind patriotism. In contrast, Sgt. Barry Sadler's ballad portrays the Green Berets as elite warriors who heroically fight and die for freedom.*

2. According to Alex Forman in "Hippies," what type of world did the hippies hope to create? *Answers will vary. Forman shares the dream of "an alternative society" in which people would live communally, sharing to insure that there was enough to go around, and people could enjoy life instead of being trapped in a search for possessions.*

3. How does Rico's Mexican heritage affect his decisions in the story "Village"? *Answers will vary. Like his ancestors, Rico's decisions are based on instinct and intuition. His decision to protect the people of Mai Cao is based on his sense that the villagers are peaceful, such as the people in the barrio where he grew up. This intuitive bonding convinces Rico that the villagers are innocent people, not the enemy.*

4. What do the poems "Farmer Nguyen" and "A Nun in Ninh Hoa" tell you about Vietnamese attitudes toward the war? *Answers will vary. Farmer Nguyen's political opinions are never mentioned; he is presented as someone who is victimized by both sides. The nun's death, like that of more than 100 Buddhist monks and nuns, may be seen as a protest against the suffering the war brought to her people.*

5. Why does the narrator of "A Piece of My Heart" build up walls? *Answers will vary. Auger is an inexperienced nurse who is unprepared to deal with the stream of casualties she can't "put back together again." She uses distance to protect herself from "losing her cool" with the severely injured people she treats.*

Writing Activity: Spinning the News

The handout on page 32 provides a graphic organizer to help students with the writing activity. You may also wish to use the Writing Activity Handout as an assessment. See also page 62 for a sample rubric to use with student projects. Answers will vary. Some possible answers follow.

1. *Hawk: Aggressive North Vietnamese Fire on American Ship; Dove: Generals Investigate Alleged Attack on American Ship*
2. *Hawk: Hippies Invade Haight-Ashbury; Dove: Hippies Promote Peace and Share the Wealth*
3. *Hawk: Private Shoots Superior in Battle Crisis; Dove: Private Saves Village from Extermination*
4. *Hawk: Little Evidence Supports Atrocity Claim; Dove: American Soldiers Slaughter Innocent Civilians*

Writing Activity: Spinning the News

Directions: As Americans realized there would be no quick victory in Vietnam, both hawks (who supported military action) and doves (who supported peaceful solutions) sought to influence public opinion. Headlines and news reports were the weapons in this war of words and images. For example, doves would emphasize the cost of the war by showing casualties and destruction. Hawks, on the other hand, tended to emphasize American military victories. Select three or four incidents from the chart below and write two headlines for each. One headline should emphasize the hawks' perspective; one should emphasize the doves' point of view. An example has been done for you.

Incident	Hawk's Headline	Dove's Headline
Example: Tet Offensive 1968	*Invasion from the north defeated*	*146 American lives lost in Tet Offensive*
U.S. Navy destroyer *Maddox* said to be attacked by North Vietnamese PT boats		
Hippies setting up a free store and a commune in San Francisco		
Rico shooting Sergeant Keever to prevent a village from being destroyed		
Hugh Thompson's decision to report the massacre at My Lai		

Remember, a strong headline
- is short.
- highlights the main topic or issue of the story.
- uses strong action verbs (*strikes, upholds, defends*).
- uses the present tense.

Cluster Two Vocabulary Test

Pages 50–77

Choose the meaning of the bold word in each passage.

1. Everybody [in Haight-Asbury was] breaking free of **conventional** morality. (*"Hippies," p. 53*)

   Ⓐ countercultural   Ⓒ traditional
   Ⓑ conflicted   Ⓓ idealistic

2. That was the illusion of the whole hippie **ethos,** that there was this abundance. (*"Hippies," p. 55*)

   Ⓐ set of values   Ⓒ type of dress
   Ⓑ way of working   Ⓓ doubt

3. They were in real **scarcity,** you know, they needed money . . . (*"Hippies," p. 55*)

   Ⓐ community   Ⓒ excess
   Ⓑ poverty   Ⓓ confusion

4. It was a **discord** not to be believed by instinct or intuition. (*"Village," p. 59*)

   Ⓐ conflict   Ⓒ harmony
   Ⓑ order   Ⓓ condition

5. Theirs was a world of . . . **intuitive** decisions. (*"Village," p. 59*)

   Ⓐ rational   Ⓒ informed
   Ⓑ slow   Ⓓ instinctive

6. My Lai was a wartime **atrocity**. (*"The Massacre at My Lai," p. 67*)

   Ⓐ victory   Ⓒ defeat
   Ⓑ mistake   Ⓓ outrage

7. My Lai . . . was pure, **premeditated** murder. (*"The Massacre at My Lai," p. 68*)

   Ⓐ planned   Ⓒ savage
   Ⓑ accidental   Ⓓ outrageous

8. We felt like we were **invincible**. (*"A Piece of My Heart," p. 71*)

   Ⓐ unknown   Ⓒ unwilling
   Ⓑ unconquerable   Ⓓ unsure

9. I got to realizing how **vulnerable** everybody was. (*"A Piece of My Heart," p. 74*)

   Ⓐ strong   Ⓒ fearless
   Ⓑ unprotected   Ⓓ invincible

10. One of my most **traumatic** and long-lasting experiences happened to me while working the POW ward. (*"A Piece of My Heart," p. 76*)

    Ⓐ uplifting   Ⓒ disturbing
    Ⓑ memorable   Ⓓ important

CLUSTER THREE

Generalizing

I. Present this definition to students.

Generalizing is drawing broad conclusions based on several pieces of specific evidence.

NOTE: While generalizing is an important thinking skill, there is a danger of assuming that generalizations are always true. Generalizations can become superstitions or stereotypes and cause us to misunderstand or misjudge things around us—see the last examples in number II below. Introduce or review the idea of stereotypes, giving more examples.

II. Discuss with students how they already use generalizing by sharing the situations below.

- You learn that over half the students in your school have experienced divorce. While only a few of your parents' classmates had divorced parents, you could generalize that divorce has become more common nationwide.

- You realize that five girls in your class have the name Tiffany and four boys have the name Taylor. From this you could generalize that Tiffany and Taylor are popular names.

- You notice that several popular singing groups are made up of all males or all females. You could generalize that music is divided along gender lines.

You might ask students to suggest other situations where they already use generalizing. Also point out how generalizing can be misused by sharing false generalizations such as those below. Point out that false generalizations either make blanket statements or are based on inadequate information.

- You know a girl who is afraid of snakes. You might falsely generalize that all girls are afraid of snakes.

- Your brothers are very interested in computers. You might falsely generalize that all boys are interested in new technologies.

III. Explain to students that they will use the selections in Cluster Three to refine their generalizations about issues related to Vietnam and the 60s. Use the following steps to show how to generalize.

A. Use the reproducible "What Happened at Home" on the next page as an overhead transparency or blackline master.

B. Review the directions with students and discuss the sample refined generalization.

C. After students complete the chart, have them identify topics on which their opinions changed. Ask them to give the facts or insights that led them to refine their initial opinions.

What Happened at Home?

Cluster Question: What was happening back home?

Generalizing is drawing broad conclusions based on several pieces of specific evidence.

Directions: The chart below lists several topics related to Vietnam and the 60s. Before you read any selections in this cluster, complete the second column by writing your general opinion about each topic based on your own experience and knowledge. If you have little or no background with a topic, put down any words or phrases you associate with the topic. After you complete writing your generalizations in column two, read the selections in cluster three of *Times of Change: Vietnam and the 60s.*

After you finish reading, use the third column to expand or amend your understanding of the topic. Your refined generalizations should reflect a new or deeper understanding of each topic, as in the example below. Be prepared to use examples from your reading to support your refined generalizations.

Topic	Initial Opinion or Generalization	Refined Generalization
Protesters	*Antiwar protesters used gentle "flower power" to express their message of nonviolence.*	*While many antiwar protests were peaceful, some radicals took "revolutionary" actions such as disrupting the 1968 Chicago Democratic Convention and burning university buildings.*
Hippies		
Student Protests		
Establishment responses to student protest		
The Generation Gap		
Government's conduct of the war		
Returning veterans		

As you read the rest of this anthology, be sure to refine your understanding and generalizations as you practiced in this activity.

Cluster Three Vocabulary

Watch for the following words as you read the selections in Cluster Three. Record your own vocabulary words and definitions on the blank lines.

San Francisco pages 80–81

vibration emotional atmosphere; overall mood or feeling

_____

_____

Law and Order Chicago Style pages 82–84

abstractedly absent-mindedly; in a preoccupied way
avowed admitted; stated
in retrospect in review; in memory
raucous disorderly; rowdy

_____

_____

Like a Rolling Stone pages 85–87

biases prejudices; one-sided views
dictate control; prescribe; impose
irrevocably irreversibly; permanently
kowtow submit; fawn

_____

_____

Woodstock Nation and **Woodstock: The Oral History** pages 88–93

archetypical model; exemplary
avant-garde pioneers; leading edge
condoned pardoned; approved
cynical distrustful; skeptical
en masse altogether; in a body
enveloped surrounded; wrapped up
hypocrisy pretense; sham
nostalgia a longing for the past
radicalized converted to extreme views; made into a political reformer
surreal bizarre; out-of-the-ordinary; fantastic
utopian ideal; visionary

_____

_____

State of Emergency at "The People's Republic of Berkeley" pages 94–97

boycott refuse to deal with; staying away
deprivation loss; dispossession
legions armies; crowds
precedent example; prototype
precursor forerunner; sign
respite break; lull; breather
skirmishes clashes; run-ins; brushes

_____

_____

Cambodia pages 98–99

blatant obvious; brazen
conciliatory pacifying; accommodating
sanctuaries safe places; hideouts
scrupulously carefully; painstakingly
Vietnamization turning over the war effort to the South Vietnamese army

_____

_____

The Kent State Tragedy pages 100–102

incensed enraged; maddened; infuriated

_____

_____

Born on the Fourth of July pages 103–107

denounced condemned; censured
legion army; multitude
maimed crippled

_____

_____

San Francisco by John Phillips, pages 80–81

Song Lyrics

Summary

This song, originally written to set a peaceful tone for the 1967 Monterey Pop Festival, became a homecoming song for Vietnam veterans who returned to the United States through San Francisco.

Reading Hint	Thinking Skill	Extension
Tell students that this song was written for the 250,000 young people expected to attend the 1967 Monterey Pop Festival.	*Generalize* about how this song reflects the 60s.	**Top 10 Songs of the 60s:** The hit song "San Francisco" expresses some values of the 60s. Have students compile a list of the top 10 songs that express the variety of values of the 90s.

Vocabulary

vibration emotional atmosphere; overall mood or feeling

Discussing the Song Lyrics

1. How does the song describe San Francisco? (Recall) *The city is a peaceful and loving place where "gentle people wear flowers in their hair."*

2. What do you think the speaker means by "a strange vibration"? (Analysis) *Answers will vary. During the 60s, young people protested against traditional values, such as materialism and unthinking patriotism, and developed a new culture based on peace, sharing, and experience of life (often enhanced by drugs). Their values offered a "new explanation" of the meaning of life and the workings of society.*

3. "I-Feel-Like-I'm-Fixin'-to-Die Rag" and "San Francisco" are both songs of the 60s, yet they have very different messages. Explain the differences. (Analysis) *Answers will vary. "I Feel Like I'm Fixin'-to-Die Rag" is an antiwar song that uses sarcasm and "GI humor" to issue a protest and demand action—an end to the war. "San Francisco," on the other hand, is pro-peace.*

Literary Focus: Symbols of the 60s

A *symbol* is an object that stands for a more abstract idea or concept. For example, in the song "San Francisco" the flower takes on the meaning of peace and loving kindness.

Have students compile a glossary of symbols used during the 60s. Their glossary might include symbols of peace as well as war. Interested students may want to compile symbols from youth culture today as a way to compare their own era with the 60s.

Law and Order Chicago Style by Donald Kaul, pages 82–84   Essay

Summary

Journalist Donald Kaul reports on his firsthand experience with the Chicago police during antiwar protests at the 1968 Democratic Convention.

Reading Hint	Thinking Skill	Extension
Build context by telling students that 100,000 protesters were expected in Chicago. Among the injured were 119 police officers, 100 protesters, and 17 journalists.	Have students decide which position they think Kaul supported: hawk or dove. Have them produce evidence from the essay to support their choice.	**Law and Order or Free Speech:** Have students choose roles as protesters, police officers, journalists, and convention delegates, and debate the following prompt: "In times of crisis, law and order is more important than free expression."

Vocabulary

abstractedly absent-mindedly; in a preoccupied way

avowed admitted; stated

in retrospect in review; in memory

raucous disorderly; rowdy

Discussing the Essay

1. What is the author's opinion of Mayor Daley's reaction to the antiwar protests at the 1968 Democratic Convention? (Recall) *Kaul considers Daley's response an "incredible" overreaction that unleashed massive police strength against outnumbered protesters and "turned Chicago into a police state."*

2. What evidence does the author give to back up his opinion? (Analysis) *Answers will vary. He describes a confrontation between 200 police officers and 100 hippies, the clearing of Lincoln Park with tear gas and clubs as reserve officers chanted "Kill!", and the harassment he and two other journalists experienced.*

3. Evaluate whether Kaul's account is balanced. (Analysis) *Answers will vary. Those who know Kaul's writing might consider him biased, because the columnist calls himself a liberal. However, his portrayal is not one-sided. The protesters are described as disorderly, hostile, and "snarling, bottle-throwing hippies." He cites incidents of police brutality,*

but also mentions two officers who intervene to stop another from harassing him.

4. What did you learn about the 60s from this selection? (Recall) *Answers will vary. Students might not have realized how militant the protests became or how deep the tensions between the generations were.*

Literary Focus: Satire

In *satire,* the faults of people or institutions are held up to ridicule. Use the following prompts to discuss Kaul's use of satire in this essay.

- Who is the main target of Kaul's satire? *The Chicago police.*
- Are other people or institutions satirized? If so, whom? *The hippies, correspondents, even Kaul himself.*
- Locate several examples of Kaul's satire in this article: *. . . it [Law and Order] was no worse than being tarred and feathered and ridden out of town on a rail. . . . whenever the cops went headhunting, which was often, there simply weren't enough hippies to go around. . . . "That's strange," I said to myself, "I thought the buses were on strike."*

About the Author: Donald Kaul

Donald Kaul's gentle brand of satire earned him a nomination for the Pulitzer Prize for distinguished commentary in 1999. Before his retirement, the syndicated columnist wrote about politics and national issues for the *Des Moines Register.*

Like a Rolling Stone   by Ben Fong-Torres, pages 85–87   Memoir

Summary

A young Chinese American editor at *Rolling Stone* finds himself unable to talk to his parents about the social and cultural revolutions he covers.

Reading Hint	Thinking Skill	Extension
Tell students to read to discover the "gap" between the author and his parents.	Ask students to use Fong-Torres' experience to make generalizations about the generation gap in the 60s.	**Generation Gaps:** Have students explore Fong-Torres' parents' point of view by asking them to act out a dialogue between his mother and father after a visit from him.

Vocabulary

biases prejudices; one-sided views

dictate control; prescribe; impose

irrevocably irreversibly; permanently

kowtow submit; fawn

Discussing the Memoir

1. Give an example of an issue that the author feels he cannot talk to his parents about. (Recall) *He doesn't talk about his work at* Rolling Stone, *or "politics, the war, civil rights, and what young people were thinking."*

2. Why does the author criticize his parents' generation? (Analysis) *Answers will vary. He feels his parents are only concerned with how things look to their peers and that they don't care about what young people are thinking or how the world is changing. He judges them as well-meaning but racist and preoccupied with* seet-meen, *or loss of face.*

3. How does the author explain his need to be different from his parents? (Analysis) *Answers will vary. Fong-Torres says he would honor their wishes if he could do so and still be true to himself. However, he wants to live in a world where cultural and racial differences are appreciated, not sources of judgment and misunderstanding.*

Special Focus: The Ideal of Equality

People growing up in the 60s became used to rapid and sweeping social change. Civil Rights activists participated in nonviolent campaigns to end separate seating for blacks and whites on buses and at lunch counters. In 1963, 200,000 people participated in the nonviolent March on Washington. In 1964, federal legislation ended discrimination against minority voters and desegregated public facilities and public education.

These questions will help students explore what Fong-Torres calls a "cultural revolution."

- Contrast the way Fong-Torres and his parents think about race.
- Why does Fong-Torres describe his parents' generation as "racist?"
- What influence do you think growing up during the Civil Rights Movement had on Fong-Torres' views about race?

Woodstock Nation by Marc Aronson and
Woodstock: The Oral History by Irwin Unger, pages 88–93

Essay/Interviews

Summary

These two pieces deal with the same topic: the Woodstock festival. In the first essay, Marc Aronson waxes eloquent on the main aspirations of the generation that produced the festival. In the second selection, Irwin Unger presents first-person accounts of several people who experienced Woodstock. The vocabulary and activities below address both selections.

Reading Hint	Thinking Skill	Extension
Have students read both selections before addressing the questions and activities below.	These two selections present very different views of Woodstock. Which do you think is the most accurate?	**Party or Protest:** Have students take positions for or against the following debate topic: Woodstock was more of a party than a protest.

Vocabulary

archetypical model; exemplary

avant-garde pioneers; leading edge

condoned pardoned; approved

cynical distrustful; skeptical

en masse altogether; in a body

enveloped surrounded; wrapped up

hypocrisy pretense; sham

nostalgia a longing for the past

radicalized converted to extreme views; made into a political reformer

surreal bizarre; out-of-the-ordinary; fantastic

utopian ideal; visionary

Discussing the Essay and the Interviews

1. Why does Marc Aronson consider Woodstock "the symbol of the peace-and-love sixties"? (Analysis) *Answers will vary. The author believes that at Woodstock a generation of young people discovered the power of peace and love for the first time. For Aronson, the festival was "the triumph of freedom" as the seekers of a new order abandoned society's rules and lived their dream of a new society.*

2. Do you think the people interviewed by Irwin Unger share Aronson's view of Woodstock? (Analysis) *Answers will vary.*

Most students will probably point out that the participants interviewed seemed as interested in having a good time as in changing the world.

Special Focus: Utopia or Dystopia

A *utopia* is a vision of a perfect world; a *dystopia* is just the opposite, an imaginary place where people lead fearful lives. In some utopian literature, planned utopias quickly degenerate into dystopias. Use the following prompts to open a discussion on the notion of Woodstock as a hippie utopia.

- In what way(s) was Woodstock a utopian experiment?
- Do you think the festival lived up to the promise of the promotional poster shown on page 91: "Woodstock: Three days of peace and music . . . and love"? Why or why not?
- Do any details in the interviews contradict the details in the Aronson essay? Explain.
- In your opinion, was Woodstock utopian or dystopian? Use details from one or both of the selections to support your opinion.
- Some people condemn Woodstock, stating that it was too idealistic. What do you think is more important, idealism or practicality? Explain your position.

State of Emergency at "The People's Republic of Berkeley" Memoir
by Tom Hayden, pages 94–97

Summary

May 15, 1969, the day that Berkeley police cleared People's Park, became known as "Bloody Thursday." During a clash between 250 armed police officers and 3,000 protesters, one man was blinded and another mortally wounded. In the aftermath, Governor Reagan declared a state of emergency and sent 2,200 National Guardsmen to Berkeley.

Reading Hint	Thinking Skill	Extension
Build context by telling students the author was a leader of Berkeley's radical Students for a Democratic Society (SDS), which promoted militant protest tactics imitated across the nation.	How might one of the leaders of the university have remembered the events presented in this memoir?	**A Radical Change:** Ask students to compare the Berkeley protesters in 1969 to the "hippies" in 1967.

Vocabulary

boycott refuse to deal with; stay away

deprivation loss; dispossession

legions armies; crowds

precedent example; prototype

precursor forerunner; sign

respite break; lull; breather

skirmishes clashes; run-ins; brushes

Discussing the Memoir

1. What sparked the protest over People's Park? (Recall) *Police fenced in a park which students and others had created on university land.*

2. What do you think People's Park represented to the protesters? to the University? the police? (Analysis) *Answers will vary. According to Hayden, the park began as a nonviolent way to oppose the university's planned development of a mall. It became a symbol of community and victory over the system. The university viewed the occupation of the park as trespassing, and the police felt compelled to enforce law and order against "the Commies" who were seizing university land for public use.*

3. Why does Hayden believe that this protest paved the way for the shootings at Kent State? (Analysis) *Answers will vary. For the first time, deadly force was used to quell a student protest, which Hayden believes set a "murderous precedent." He also cites officials who believed that deadly force was an appropriate response to the confrontations that students provoked.*

Special Focus: A Spectrum of Protest

Before 1967, antiwar protests were peaceful. Then some radicals adopted militant tactics: shouting down speakers who disagreed with them, organizing protests at the 1968 Chicago Democratic Convention, and planting 5,000 bombs between 1967 and 1970.

Put a line on the board, with *pro-war* on one end and *militant radical* on the other. Place Tom Hayden, who helped organize the Chicago protests, toward the radical end of the spectrum. Then ask students to place people in other selections on the continuum. Discuss what might cause a person to move from the middle toward either extreme.

Cambodia by President Richard M. Nixon, pages 98–99   Speech

Summary

In this speech, President Nixon presents the government's decision to send troops into Cambodia to destroy North Vietnamese military headquarters located there.

Reading Hint	Thinking Skill	Extension
Note: the speech that is presented here has been shortened.	Have students look at the map on page 11 to determine why Cambodia became involved in the war.	**The Pundits Respond:** Have students act the part of political commentators reviewing Nixon's speech. Have them summarize the main points of his speech and predict how hawks and doves will react to the government's plans.

Vocabulary

blatant obvious; brazen

conciliatory pacifying; accommodating

sanctuaries safe places; hideouts

scrupulously carefully; painstakingly

Vietnamization turning over the war effort to the South Vietnamese army

Discussing the Speech

1. Describe the "strong and effective measures" President Nixon announces in this speech. (Recall) *American troops are being sent to fight with the South Vietnamese armies attacking Communist strongholds in Cambodia.*

2. How does the president attempt to convince the American people he is doing the right thing? (Analysis) *Answers will vary. He describes a buildup of Viet Cong forces along the border and argues that this action will protect American lives and promote peace by bringing a quick end to the war. He promises to continue participation in the peace talks. He also appeals to American pride and the desire to remain a first-rate, undefeated world power.*

3. How do you think the president expects Americans to react to his decision? (Analysis) *Answers will vary. He seems to anticipate that the decision to extend the war into Cambodia could cost him re-election. However, he hopes that people will appreciate that he is not thinking about popularity, but doing what he thinks is right.*

Special Focus: Cambodia

After the deposition of the pro-American Prince Sihanouk in March, 1970, civil war broke out in Cambodia. The victors were the Khmer Rouge, communist guerrillas who tried to create a utopian communist state. All institutions, including schools, churches, hospitals, and families, were banned. People who lived in the cities were relocated to the country and forced to work in the fields 12-14 hours a day. During this reign of terror, more than two million people died by starvation, torture, or execution on the "killing fields." When North Vietnam conquered the country in 1979, Cambodia had lost 30% of its population in one of the worst genocides in history.

The Kent State Tragedy by Roger Barr, pages 100–102   Article

Summary

A series of protests sparked by President Nixon's Cambodia speech led to the burning of Kent State's ROTC Building and the calling out of the Ohio National Guard. Four days after the protests began, thirteen seconds of rifle fire left four students dead and nine wounded.

Reading Hint	Thinking Skill	Extension
Have students notice how this short article flows smoothly from its introduction to a chronology of events and a final historical conclusion.	In what way was the Kent State tragedy a turning point in America's involvement in Vietnam?	**Summing It Up:** Ask students to write a caption for the photograph on page 102.

Vocabulary

incensed enraged; maddened; infuriated

Discussing the Article

1. What caused the 1970 protests at Kent State? (Recall) *The protests began in response to President Nixon's announcement that American troops were taking part in attacks against enemy sanctuaries in Cambodia.*

2. Why did the protests turn violent? (Analysis) *Answers will vary. The burning of the ROTC building brought the Ohio National Guard to campus. As each attempt to bring order to the campus was met by defiance, antagonism between students and Guardsmen increased. Students threw rocks and tear gas canisters at the Guard. The Guard attempted to disperse the protesters with tear gas, bayonets, and, tragically, rifle fire.*

3. What connection does the author make between the deaths at Kent State and the war in Vietnam? (Analysis) *Answers will vary. The author believes these "unnecessary and senseless deaths" contributed to the growing sense that American lives were being wasted in Vietnam and swayed public sympathy toward the protesters rather than the government.*

Special Focus: Questions About Kent State

Students may have these questions about the tragedy at Kent State.

- How did the protests begin? *The first protest was small and peaceful. However, afterwards some students broke windows in downtown Kent. Police used tear gas and made 15 arrests. Fearing further disturbances, city and university officials decided to call in the Ohio National Guard.*

- Why did the Guard use lethal force? *The reason the Guard opened fire is not clear. Some of the students killed were not even involved in the protest. However, tensions between students and the Guard had been increasing for two days. Survivor Ron Stamps, who believes the shooting was premeditated, wants another investigation.*

- How did Americans respond to the deaths at Kent State? *Students at over 700 colleges participated in a nationwide student strike that caused many colleges to end their spring sessions early. Some Americans supported the students' right to protest, while others insisted on the need for law and order. Outrage at the students' deaths increased public pressure to end American involvement in Vietnam.*

Born on the Fourth of July by Ron Kovic, pages 103–107   Autobiography

Summary

Ex-Marine Ron Kovic was paralyzed from the waist down after being shot in the shoulder in Vietnam. Poor treatment in a Veterans' Hospital and the shootings at Kent State begin his conversion into an antiwar activist.

Reading Hint	Thinking Skill	Extension
Ask students to trace the transformation of a decorated Marine into an antiwar activist.	Ron Kovic told the 1976 Democratic Convention: "I am the living death/the memorial day on wheels." Explore what he means by this statement.	**The Meaning of Patriotism:** Ask students to decide whether Ron Kovic was more patriotic as a Marine or as a war protester.

Vocabulary

denounced condemned; censured

legion army; multitude

maimed crippled

Discussing the Autobiography

1. What is Ron Kovic's reaction when he first hears about the antiwar protests? (Recall) *As a soldier in Vietnam, he feels disbelief and anger that people would protest against men risking their lives for their country. He considers the protesters traitors.*

2. Contrast Kovic's feelings about the first and second protests he takes part in. (Analysis) *Answers will vary. At the first rally, Kovic describes himself as a supportive "observer" who is reluctant to get fully involved. In Washington, no longer an observer, Kovic feels that he and his fellow protesters are part of a healing community.*

3. What causes the change in Kovic's attitude toward protest? (Analysis) *Answers will vary. The poor treatment he received in a Veterans' Hospital causes him to lose faith in the war, but he doesn't participate in any protests until he needs to respond to the shootings at Kent State. In Washington, the police attack on the crowd shocks him. The sense of community he experiences makes him feel that he is "never going to be the same" and inspires him to work for healing.*

Literary Focus: Turning Points

At the beginning of this excerpt Ron Kovic is an avowed supporter of the war effort; by the end he is an avid antiwar protester. Have students map the main events that caused Kovic to change his position.

About the Author: Ron Kovic

Ron Kovic (1946–) served in Vietnam from 1964–1968, coming home with medals and a shoulder wound that paralyzed him from the waist down. Disillusioned by memories such as destroying a village in which no one had been armed and by being thrown away to "rot in VA hospitals," Kovic became an antiwar activist.

Kovic's book is the basis of Oliver Stone's 1991 movie *Born on the Fourth of July*, with Tom Cruise starring as Kovic. The ex-Marine's wish to be a hero has been achieved through his work for peace and his advocacy for veterans.

What Was Happening Back Home?

Thinking Skill GENERALIZING

1. There was an immediate and overwhelming reaction of disbelief and outrage after Nixon's Cambodia speech. Why do you think this was so? Explain your answer. *Answers will vary. Some may point out, as Nixon does, that he had just ordered the withdrawal of 150,000 troops from Vietnam. His announcement of his decision to broaden the war seemed to contradict his earlier action. Such contradictions may have confused citizens and caused them to doubt the promises of their leaders.*

2. What do you think Woodstock represented to America's youth and to the establishment? **Compare and contrast** the reactions. Answers will vary. *For members of the younger generation, Woodstock would have represented a chance for them to express their ideals of peace and freedom. For the establishment, Woodstock would have represented anarchy.*

3. The phrase "generation gap" was coined during the 1960s to describe the growing distrust and misunderstanding between the youthful counterculture and the older generation or establishment. Use a chart such as the one below to gather details about both sides of the generation gap. Then use the details to write a **general statement** about each side. Be sure to base your generalizations on specific details. *Answers will vary. Here are some suggested answers.*

Selection	Characteristics of Establishment	Characteristics of Counterculture
"Law & Order Chicago Style"	brutal; rude; believed in the war; believed in law and order; threatened bystanders	chanted obscenities; waved Viet Cong flags; littered; wore long hair; went barefoot; camped in the park; planned disruption
"Like a Rolling Stone"	*judge people on surface appearances; afraid of losing face; uninterested in what young people think; racist*	*long-haired; interested in Civil Rights; experiencing a social and cultural revolution; not rebellious but committed to an ideal of equality*
"Woodstock Nation/Woodstock: The Oral History"	*driven; materialistic; repressed; hypocritical; boring*	*radicalized; wearing beads, headbands, and tie-dye; visionary; bedraggled; powerful; permissive; free; avant-garde*
"A State of Emergency . . ."	*hard-line; uses deadly force*	*revolutionary; angered*
"Born on the Fourth of July"	*frightened; angry; brutal*	*nonviolent; free; sharing; committed to peace and healing*
Generalization	*The establishment was satisfied with the status quo and responded to revolutionary tactics by enforcing law and order.*	*Members of the counterculture lived their alternative vision in ways ranging from rock festivals to violent protest.*

4. Why do you think the authorities in Chicago, Berkeley, and Kent State reacted strongly to the protesters? *Answers will vary. In each case, authorities saw a threat to law and order. Chicago protesters planned to disrupt the 1969 Democratic Convention, Berkeley students had taken over university land, and Kent State students burned down the ROTC building. Authorities may have overreacted to show that they could maintain order and protect property and because of increasing hostility between the two sides, with law enforcement seeing the hippies as "Commies" and protesters taunting and injuring police.*

Writing Activity: Dueling Letters to the Editor

The handout on page 46 provides a graphic organizer to help students with the writing activity. You may also wish to use the Writing Activity Handout as an assessment. See also page 62 for a sample rubric to use with student projects.

Writing Activity: Dueling Letters to the Editor

Directions Readers of newspapers often vent their emotions by writing letters to the editor. With a partner, chose one of the incidents in this cluster. Each of you will write a letter to the editor about the incident, with one of you taking the side of the counterculture and the other taking the side of the establishment.

The organizer below will help you develop ideas for your letters. First select one of the incidents that you and your partner are interested in. Then choose a side. Briefly outline "your" view on the incident and develop a generalization that states your opinion. Then give clear reasons for your opinion. Use facts instead of overgeneralizations such as "*All* police react brutally to protesters, who are *always* nonviolent." End by restating the opinion you want readers to remember.

Incident	Counterculture's view	Establishment's view
1. Protests at the 1969 Chicago Democratic Convention		
2. Civil Rights Movement		
3. Woodstock Festival		
4. Conflict at the University of Berkeley		
5. Expansion of the war into Cambodia		
6. Shooting of Kent State students		
7. May 9, 1970, march on Washington		

Use your strongest opinions and evidence in your letters to the editor. Remember, a strong editorial
- begins with a general statement based on facts.
- states your opinion.
- lists clear reasons for your opinion.
- avoids overgeneralization and universal terms such as all, always, and never.
- ends with a summary of your opinion.

Cluster Three Vocabulary Test

Pages 80–107

Vocabulary Words

Choose the meaning of the bold word in each passage.

1. All across the nation /
   Such a strange **vibration**.
   (*"San Francisco," p. 80*)

   Ⓐ shaking   Ⓒ mood
   Ⓑ earthquake   Ⓓ sensation

2. . . . I followed some **raucous** hippies down
   Michigan Avenue . . .
   (*"Law and Order Chicago Style," p. 83*)

   Ⓐ peaceful   Ⓒ dirty
   Ⓑ quiet   Ⓓ disorderly

3. Here I am, an editor at a magazine
   chronicling . . . the massive social and
   cultural revolutions that are **irrevocably**
   changing our world.
   (*"Like a Rolling Stone," p. 87*)

   Ⓐ rapidly   Ⓒ permanently
   Ⓑ dangerously   Ⓓ unavoidably

4. That kind of submission, I said, fostered
   perpetual racism and other **biases**.
   (*"Like a Rolling Stone," p. 87*)

   Ⓐ crimes   Ⓒ gatherings
   Ⓑ prejudices   Ⓓ memorials

5. To this day, whether as **nostalgia** or satire,
   Woodstock remains the symbol of the peace-
   and-love sixties.
   (*"Woodstock Nation," p. 89*)

   Ⓐ longing for home   Ⓒ longing for hope
   Ⓑ longing for peace   Ⓓ longing for the past

6. A generation that would not put up with old
   lies, **hypocrisy**, and boredom was demonstrating its alternative vision of how people
   could live and love. (*"Woodstock Nation,"
   p. 90*)

   Ⓐ ignorance   Ⓒ idealism
   Ⓑ pretense   Ⓓ stereotypes

7. . . . the murderous **precedent** was
   established. (*"State of Emergency at 'The
   People's Republic of Berkeley'," p. 97*)

   Ⓐ example   Ⓒ excuse
   Ⓑ argument   Ⓓ claim

8. This key control center has been occupied by
   the North Vietnamese and Vietcong for 5
   years in **blatant** violation of Cambodia's
   neutrality. (*"Cambodia," p. 99*)

   Ⓐ secret   Ⓒ joint
   Ⓑ planned   Ⓓ obvious

9. . . . we will be **conciliatory** at the conference
   table . . . (*"Cambodia," p. 99*)

   Ⓐ stubborn   Ⓒ pacifying
   Ⓑ angry   Ⓓ humble

10. Many of us would not be coming back and
    many others would be wounded or **maimed**.
    (*"Born on the Fourth of July," p. 103*)

    Ⓐ killed   Ⓒ sick
    Ⓑ crippled   Ⓓ disillusioned

Teaching Cluster Four

The final cluster in *Times of Change: Vietnam and the 60s* can be presented using one or more of the following methods.

- presented by the teacher
- used for independent student learning
- used for a final assessment

Use the chart below to plan.

Teacher Presentation	Independent Learning/Assessment
For teacher-directed study you can • pass out cluster vocabulary sheet. • set schedule for reading selections. • use appropriate discussion questions and extension activities for each selection. • administer vocabulary test. • assign research projects. • administer final essay test.	**Students can** • plan and present a lesson over one or more of the selections in the last cluster. • prepare a vocabulary study sheet and create and administer a vocabulary test. • conduct additional research on a related topic. • respond to one or more of the questions or activities on the Responding to Cluster Four page.

Teacher Notes

CLUSTER FOUR

Synthesizing

I. Present this definition to students.

Synthesizing means combining parts into a new whole.

II. Discuss with students how they already use synthesis by sharing the following situations.

You synthesize when you

- use what you already know to figure out the meaning of a new word.
- combine several brainstorming suggestions to develop a solution to a problem.
- develop a consensus of opinion based on everyone's ideas.
- use information from several different sources in a project.
- adapt an idea from one form to another (for example, you create a play based on a novel or a dance based on a poem).

You might ask students to suggest other situations where synthesizing would be used.

III. Use the following steps to show students how to synthesize.

A. Give students copies of the handout on the next page. (Or use it as an overhead for a class discussion and synthesis activity.)

B. Explain to students that the handout will help them synthesize their ideas about the essential question: What effect did the decade of the 60s have on the United States?

C. Have students complete the organizer according to the directions and the examples given.

D. If you wish to take the activity one step further, have students compile their ideas into a class list. Have students identify the most important events and issues of the 60s. Then work with them to generate a class statement about the lasting influence of these times of change.

Times of Change—A Synthesis

Synthesizing: In **synthesizing,** you combine or rearrange statements, feelings, or ideas to provide a new or fresh perspective on a topic.

Directions: The chart below will help you organize your ideas about how the 60s changed America. In the first column, identify the most important events and issues of the decade. Consider trends (such as fashion), issues (such as the generation gap), values (such as freedom), music (such as protest songs), and popular opinion (such as distrust of government). In the second column, describe the way each event or issue changed American society. Note: there can be more than one way an event such as the Vietnam War influenced society. Finally, **synthesize** your ideas into a final statement about the lasting influence of the 60s. Before you write your final statement, you may find it helpful to review the table of contents and the essays at the beginning of the book.

Issue or Event of the 60s	How It Changed the United States
War in Vietnam	Some in the U.S. are reluctant to get involved in conflicts abroad because of the defeat in Vietnam.

Final statement about the effect(s) the decade of the 60s had on the United States:

_____

_____

_____

_____

Cluster Four Vocabulary

Watch for the following words as you read the selections in Cluster Four. Record your own vocabulary words and definitions on the blank lines.

Where Have All the Flowers Gone?
pages 110–111

passing going by; dying

_____

_____

Epilogue pages 112–116

chaos disorder; confusion
concussion shaking; vibration
disconsolate dejected; downcast
diverted turned; deflected
epilogue afterword; concluding section
evacuation emergency departure; removal from a place of danger
exhilarating exciting; uplifting
junks boats
simulated imitated; mimicked
speculate guess
wanly bloodlessly; weakly

_____

_____

A President's Pain page 117

strategy plan; method

_____

_____

The Summer of Vietnam pages 118–119

agonized suffered; struggled
extinguish put out
machismo sense of masculine pride; sense of power
prestigious honored; respected; esteemed
proportion balance; percentage
redeemed recovered; reclaimed

_____

_____

Stop the Sun pages 120–127

foundered sank
inert inactive; still
paddy wet land in which rice is grown
syndrome group of related symptoms

_____

_____

To Heal a Nation pages 128–141

ambiguity uncertainty; doubtfulness
egomaniacs self-centered people
eloquently expressively; moving
fiasco complete failure; breakdown
inequities injustices; unfairnesses
perpetuate cause to last; immortalize
poignancy touching; piercing
potential possible; probable
proximity nearness; closeness
subside decrease; lessen; die down
transcend rise above; triumph; overcome
vulnerable unprotected; exposed

_____

_____

Where Have All the Flowers Gone? by Pete Seeger, pages 110–111   Song Lyrics

Summary

This folk-style song, sung by Joan Baez and the singing group Peter, Paul, and Mary, became an anthem of the antiwar movement.

Reading Hint	Thinking Skill	Extension
If possible, allow students to hear the song as performed by Peter, Paul, and Mary.	Ask students to *synthesize* their ideas about how this song typifies the 60s.	**The Power of Song:** Ask students to discuss how this comment by Pete Seeger applies to this song: "At best, music helps in understanding troubles and helps get people together to do something about their troubles."

Vocabulary

passing going by; dying

Discussing the Song Lyrics

1. What happens to the young men in the song? (Recall) *All of them become soldiers and die.*

2. What pattern do the lyrics follow? (Analysis) *Answers will vary. The subject introduced in the fourth line of each stanza—young girls, young men, soldiers, grave-yards—becomes the focus of the next stanza. The pattern creates a cycle of uninterrupted fighting and death.*

3. Why do you think this song became popular with those who opposed the war in Vietnam? (Analysis) *Answers will vary. The question "When will we ever learn?" suggests that peace, while difficult to achieve, is a more desirable alternative than war. The deaths of "every one" of the young men also point out the wastefulness of war. The soldiers in the song are caught in the cycle of violence, just as draftees felt caught up in a war many didn't understand.*

Special Focus: Protest Songs

The songs "Blowin' in the Wind" by Bob Dylan and "Where Have All the Flowers Gone?" by Pete Seeger typify much of the protest music of the early 1960s. Such songs became very popular and were played on radio stations across the nation. Use the following prompts to discuss the topic of protest songs then and now.

- Do you recognize any of the following protest songs: "Blowin' in the Wind," "Give Peace a Chance," "If I Had a Hammer," "We Shall Overcome"?

- Do you think that protest songs are as popular today as they were in the 60s? Why or why not?

- If you were to write a protest song today, what would it protest?

About the Song Writer: Pete Seeger

Pete Seeger's adaptation of "We Shall Overcome" became the anthem of the Civil Rights Movement. His original songs are associated with many social justice issues, including the union movement, Civil Rights, world peace, and environmental protection. Songs he wrote to protest the war in Vietnam include "Waist Deep in the Big Muddy" and "If You Love Your Uncle Sam, Bring 'Em Home."

In a 1971 interview, Seeger remarked, ". . . there must be something in protest songs or television wouldn't be so anxious to keep them off the air."

Epilogue by Philip Caputo, pages 112–116

Autobiography

Summary

Journalist Philip Caputo gives a first-person account of the 1975 evacuation of Saigon.

Reading Hint	Thinking Skill	Extension
Tell students that Saigon was the capital of South Vietnam.	Why was the evacuation of Saigon the "end of an era?"	**Graphing the Drama:** This account uses good narrative techniques to keep the reader's attention. Have students chart the narrative using a line graph, with time represented on the x axis and level of drama on the y axis.

Vocabulary

chaos disorder; confusion

concussion shaking; vibration

disconsolate dejected; downcast

diverted turned; deflected

epilogue afterword; concluding section

evacuation emergency departure; removal from a place of danger

exhilarating exciting; uplifting

junks boats

simulated imitated; mimicked

speculate guess

wanly bloodlessly; weakly

Discussing the Autobiography

1. What did the Americans in Saigon fear might happen if the Viet Cong invaded the capital? (Recall) *Caputo and his fellow Americans feared that they might be trapped in the city or shot by South Vietnamese soldiers who felt betrayed by their former allies.*

2. How does the author make the experience of the evacuation vivid for readers? (Analysis) *Answers will vary. Caputo includes many sensory details, such as the "thud" of bombs and the description of gekko lizards on the white walls. He also describes dramatic action, such as the downing of a C-199 cargo plane.*

3. What does the author see as the significance of the evacuation? (Analysis) *Answers will vary. He feels "like a deserter" as he abandons the South Vietnamese to their fate. The departure marks America's first defeat in war and the "end of an era" in which the United States dominated world affairs.*

Special Focus: The Aftermath

Students may have these questions about the evacuation and its aftermath.

- How many people were evacuated? *Nearly 9,000 people were evacuated, including 1,373 American noncombatants. The last American combatants had been withdrawn in 1973.*

- What happened after the Americans left? *Five hours after the last helicopters left, South Vietnam General Duong Van Minh ordered an end to the fighting. Saigon fell without a battle.*

  Once the Americans left, farmers forced off their land by the war had no means of support. Many, along with those fleeing political and religious persecution, became "boat people." Eventually, over 130,000 refugees were resettled.

  The region remained chaotic. After Vietnam invaded Cambodia to end the reign of the Khmer Rouge, famine struck Cambodians. A socialist government was established in Laos.

A President's Pain by President Gerald R. Ford, page 117

Vignette

Summary

In an essay on the anniversary of the fall of Saigon, President Ford recalls the final retreat from Vietnam.

Reading Hint	Thinking Skill	Extension
This selection is very short and informal. Students may have to infer President Ford's emotional state.	Ask students to *contrast* this piece with Nixon's Cambodia speech on pages 98–99.	**Comparison:** Have students compare and contrast this remembrance with Abraham Lincoln's Gettysburg Address.

Vocabulary

strategy plan; method

Discussing the Vignette

1. How does President Ford describe his role in the Vietnam conflict? (Recall) *He says that though he supported the actions of the presidents before him, ironically, he is "the president who ends up losing the war."*

2. What priorities did the president set for the evacuation? (Recall) *Answers may vary. He decided to stay until the last moment to rescue as many Americans and allies as possible.*

3. Why do you think President Ford called the final days in Vietnam "the saddest of my public life"? (Analysis) *Answers will vary. The president felt himself "torn" among conflicting advisers, suffering military humiliation, and hoping that a desperate "heroic effort" would rescue as many as possible.*

4. The evacuation of Saigon is one of Gerald Ford's most enduring memories of the Vietnam conflict. What image(s) of the conflict stand out in your mind? (Analysis) *Answers will vary. You might suggest that students review the table of contents before answering.*

Special Focus: The First U.S. Defeat

Reflecting on the Vietnam War 25 years later, columnist Donald Kaul wrote, "Not the least of the casualties was our illusion of invincibility." Use these questions to help students explore the implications of America's defeat in Vietnam.

- In his speech on Cambodia (pages 98–99), what did President Nixon see as the implications of defeat for the United States? *Nixon equated defeat with becoming a "second-rate power" and accepting humiliation in his announcement of the expansion of the war into Cambodia.*

- How did the loss of South Vietnam affect Americans' attitude toward their government? *Answers will vary. Widespread belief that the government had recklessly sent Americans to die in a fruitless civil war, along with media exposure of governmental lies, resulted in mistrust of government and a reluctance to commit American troops abroad.*

- How did the Vietnam War affect America's sense of its role in the world? *Answers will vary. Instead of seeing itself as the world's police officer and defender of democracy, the U.S. now tends to get involved in foreign conflicts only when national interests are at stake.*

The Summer of Vietnam   by Barbara Renaud González, pages 118–119   Essay

Summary

A Latina author reflects on what her people gave and lost during the Vietnam War.

Reading Hint	Thinking Skill	Extension
Tell students that in this personal essay, the author makes connections between public events and private memories.	Ask students to *compare* the way Hispanic soldiers are described in this piece and in "Village."	**The Universal Language of Grief:** Ask students to discuss what it means to "cry in Spanish."

Vocabulary

agonized suffered; struggled

extinguish put out

machismo sense of masculine pride; sense of power

prestigious honored; respected; esteemed

proportion balance; percentage

redeemed recovered; reclaimed

Discussing the Essay

1. What memory comes to mind when the author thinks of Vietnam? (Recall) *She remembers young Ernesto Sanchez, who died in combat when the author was 13 years old.*

2. How does the author's ethnic background shape her view of the war? (Analysis) *Answers will vary. She feels a close bond with her Latino "brothers-at-war." Those who died are a loss to her people. She notes that their machismo made them brave fighters. While they suffered disproportionate losses, their contributions have not been recognized by the American people at large.*

3. What do you think the author means by proposing to give a grieving mother a Purple Heart? (Analysis) *Answers will vary. Purple Hearts are given to those wounded in battle; while the mother did not fight, the loss of her son has wounded her. Her son sacrificed his life for America, but continuing discrimination makes it seem as if he "died for nothing."*

Literary Focus: Succinct and Powerful

Author González intentionally breaks some rules of standard English with short, punchy phrases presented as full sentences.

Imagined kissing them.
Always teased me.
My brothers-at-war.
First in, last out.

Use the following to prompt discussion.

- Convert these phrases, or others in the story, to traditional sentences with a subject and a verb. Are they as powerful? Explain.
- When is it acceptable to break the rules of English?
- Ask a student to read part of the essay aloud. Do they find the language González uses more powerful when it is spoken or read silently?

Stop the Sun by Gary Paulsen, pages 120–127

Short Story

Summary

Thirteen-year-old Terry wonders why his father's eyes "go away." After Terry dares to open the subject, his father shares a combat experience that made him feel dead inside. Terry resolves to continue his efforts to understand his father's pain.

Reading Hint	Thinking Skill	Extension
Have students watch for hints for the meaning of the title.	Ask students to *compare* the experiences of Mr. Erickson and Jack Smith (pages 22-31).	**Epilogue:** Ask students to speculate about what happens to the relationship between Terry and his father.

Vocabulary

foundered sank

inert inactive; still

paddy wet land in which rice is grown

syndrome group of related symptoms

Discussing the Short Story

1. What happens when Terry's father's eyes "go away"? (Recall) *Mr. Erickson is having flashbacks to Vietnam, where he was the only survivor among 54 men pinned down by enemy fire for a night.*

2. Describe how Terry's feelings toward his father change. (Analysis) *Answers will vary. At first, Terry is confused and curious. Then embarrassment leads to avoiding his father in public. After he opens a discussion with his father, Terry is afraid that he has reopened old wounds. At the end, his knowledge gives him the strength to accept his father and continue reaching out to him.*

3. Comment on whether Terry did the right thing when he asked his father about Vietnam. (Analysis) *Answers will vary. Some may argue that Terry had a right to know; others may feel he intruded on his father's privacy. The ending suggests that the question strengthened the understanding between father and son, and even created a possibility for healing.*

4. What you do think the title means? (Analysis) *Answers will vary. The title refers to Mr. Erickson's belief that he could escape being shot at first light if he could stop the dawn from coming. In a sense, his life stopped in that paddy, where he felt he "died. Inside."*

Special Focus: Posttraumatic Stress Syndrome

Posttraumatic stress syndrome—characterized by depression, anxiety, flashbacks, and night-mares—affects up to 30 percent of those who served in Vietnam, including combat veterans and nurses.

Combat stress is not unique to this war. However, the average age of those serving in Vietnam was 19, younger than those in previous wars. In addition, soldiers often did not have a chance to develop close bonds with their units, and they received no help making the transition to life at home.

- Help students identify the posttraumatic stress experienced by Anne Auger (pp. 70–77), Jack Smith (pp. 22–31), and Ron Kovic (pp. 103–107).
- Discuss how the experience of these real people compares to that of Paulsen's fictional character.

About the Author: Gary Paulsen

Gary Paulsen (1939–) is recognized for his survival novels, such as *Hatchet,* and his autobiographical writings, such as *My Life in Dog Years.* Paulsen, whose own father suffered long-term effects from his World War II experience, has written several books on the theme of combat stress. *The Crossing* (1987), *The Monument* (1991), *Sentries* (1986), and *Soldier's Heart: A Novel of the Civil War* (1998).

To Heal a Nation   by Joel L. Swerdlow, pages 128–141   Article

Summary

Returning Vietnam veterans often became targets of hostility toward the war. One of them, Jan Scruggs, envisioned a memorial with the names of all the dead and those missing in action. This article tells the moving story of the building of the Vietnam Veterans Memorial, which millions have visited since its dedication in 1982.

Reading Hint	Thinking Skill	Extension
The length of this article may challenge some students. Explain to them that they may enjoy the piece more if they think of it as a narrative.	In what way(s) does the Vietnam Veterans Memorial *synthesize* the era of the 60s?	**A Comparison:** Compare and contrast the Tomb of the Unknowns (also known as the Tomb of the Unknown Soldier) to the Vietnam Veterans Memorial.

Vocabulary

ambiguity uncertainty; doubtfulness

egomaniacs self-centered people

eloquent expressive; moving

fiasco complete failure; breakdown

inequities injustices; unfairnesses

perpetuate cause to last; immortalize

poignancy touching; piercing

potential possible; probable

proximity nearness; closeness

subside decrease; lessen; die down

transcend rise above; triumph; overcome

vulnerable unprotected; exposed

Discussing the Article

1. How were veterans treated when they returned home? (Recall) *Instead of receiving a hero's welcome, veterans found their service in an unpopular war was often ignored or condemned.*

2. What aspects of the wall were controversial? (Recall) *Some opposed building a memorial to "losers" or feared that the wall would perpetuate political divisions. Debate also ensued over the abstract design, the way the names were listed, and the need for a conventional statue.*

3. How has the wall helped to heal a nation? (Analysis) *Answers may vary. Veterans no longer had to carry the burden of*

unrecognized sacrifices. While still divided about whether the war should have been fought, the nation was able to unite in mourning. Survivors found that old wounds, once reopened, could heal cleanly. Because the nation remembers, the sacrifices and the lessons of Vietnam will not be lost.

Special Focus: No Hero's Welcome

Instead of being honored by homecoming parades, veterans returning from Vietnam often received abuse. People had seen children burned by napalm and read about massacres such as My Lai. Some blamed the soldiers returning home for these horrors. Few understood or acknowledged the sacrifices made by those serving in an unpopular war.

Use these questions to help students *synthesize* their ideas about coming home from Vietnam.

- In previous wars, soldiers were portrayed as heroes. How do you think news coverage of Vietnam affected people's reaction to veterans?

- How might people have reacted differently if South Vietnam had not fallen?

- Of the people you have read about, who had the most difficult homecoming? Give reasons for your opinion.

Cluster Four Vocabulary Test

Pages 110–141

Vocabulary Words

Choose the meaning of the bold word in each passage.

1. In the final moments of **chaos,** would the South Vietnamese . . . turn their weapons on every American they saw? (*"Epilogue," p. 112*)

   Ⓐ surrender Ⓒ disorder
   Ⓑ invasion Ⓓ life

2. It was useless to **speculate** . . . (*"Epilogue," p. 112*)

   Ⓐ answer Ⓒ hope
   Ⓑ discuss Ⓓ guess

3. . . . the lead helicopter in our flight diverted [the missile] with a decoy flare that **simulated** an aircraft engine's heat. (*"Epilogue," p. 116*)

   Ⓐ imitated Ⓒ hid
   Ⓑ reduced Ⓓ used

4. I supported Johnson even though I differed on some of his military **strategy** . . . (*"A President's Pain," p. 117*)

   Ⓐ equipment Ⓒ might
   Ⓑ recruiting Ⓓ plan

5. Who would dare **extinguish** the crooked smile, football hands and Aqua Velva faces I knew so well? (*"The Summer of Vietnam," p. 119*)

   Ⓐ put off Ⓒ put away
   Ⓑ put out Ⓓ put together

6. We Latinos received more medals, thirteen of the **prestigious** Medal of Honor, than any other group. (*"The Summer of Vietnam," p. 119*)

   Ⓐ rare Ⓒ metallic
   Ⓑ esteemed Ⓓ common

7. "Anyone who died in that **fiasco** is a hero in my eyes." (*"To Heal a Nation," p. 131*)

   Ⓐ effort Ⓒ achievement
   Ⓑ cause Ⓓ failure

8. "Let's not **perpetuate** the memory of such dishonorable events by erecting monuments to them." (*"To Heal a Nation," p. 131*)

   Ⓐ erase Ⓒ stain
   Ⓑ immortalize Ⓓ forget

9. "This design seems able to capture all the feelings of **ambiguity** and anguish that the Vietnam War evoked in this nation." (*"To Heal a Nation," p. 134*)

   Ⓐ patriotism Ⓒ uncertainty
   Ⓑ protest Ⓓ anger

10. . . . the names as displayed in Maya Lin's design would speak **eloquently** of sacrifice, commitment, and patriotism . . . (*" To Heal a Nation," p. 134*)

   Ⓐ expressively Ⓒ eternally
   Ⓑ haltingly Ⓓ wisely

Research, Writing, and Discussion Topics

The following are suggested topics you might research, write about, or discuss.

1. *Summarize* the ways in which the Civil Rights Movement influenced the student protesters of the 60s.
2. *Generalize* about the influence of protest music in the 60s.
3. *Summarize* the reasons Americans became involved in the Vietnam conflict.
4. *Analyze* why student protests became increasingly violent.
5. *Synthesize* a statement of the counterculture's vision of an alternative society.
6. *Analyze* why American public opinion turned against the war.
7. Agree or disagree with this *generalization* by General Edward C. Meyer: "You can't send soldiers off to war without having the support of the American people."
8. *Analyze* which character in the book best exemplifies what it means to work for change.
9. *Analyze* the decision made by a character who had to choose between following orders or following conscience.
10. *Generalize* about how a citizen who believes his or her country is fighting an unjust war could best fulfill his or her patriotic duty.
11. *Summarize* President Ford's reasons for granting amnesty to draft evaders.
12. Give your opinion about this *generalization* by Donald Kaul: "Not the least of the casualties [of the war in Vietnam] was our illusion of invincibility."
13. *Summarize* the reasons for America's withdrawal from Vietnam.
14. *Generalize* about why the adjustment of Vietnam veterans to life after the war has been particularly difficult.
15. Agree or disagree with this *generalization* by an American army officer: "There were no victors in Vietnam—only victims."
16. *Summarize* the lessons Americans learned from Vietnam and the 60s.
17. *Analyze* which selection in the book best captures your sense of how times were changing in the 60s.

Assessment and Project Ideas

Extended Research Opportunities

Here are some topics that you may wish to investigate further and report on either in writing or in an oral presentation to the class.

- Agent Orange
- battles, such as Hamburger Hill or the Tet Offensive
- boat people and refugees
- campus violence
- the Chicago Eight
- conscientious objectors
- literature of the Vietnam War
- media coverage of the war
- minorities in the war

- music of the 60s
- Paris Peace Talks
- *Pentagon Papers*
- posttraumatic stress syndrome
- the protest movement
- veterans
- Vietnam today
- war correspondents and photographers
- women in the war
- Woodstock

Speaking and Listening

1. Write a brief speech that you might have presented to the Congressional committee deciding whether to approve the Vietnam Veterans Memorial.
2. Using poems, songs, and quotations, create a Readers Theatre that focuses on the meaning of Vietnam or the 60s today.
3. Find a poem or short excerpt related to Vietnam or the 60s and interpret it for the class. Prepare an introduction that explains why you chose this piece and what it says to you about that era.
4. Debate the following topic: Those who died in Vietnam died for nothing.
5. Write and present a short dramatic scene between someone who protested during the 60s and a young person today.
6. Create an oral history of the changes during the 60s. Interview a variety of people, including veterans, protesters, police officers, and members of "the Silent Majority."

Creative Writing

1. Write a dialogue between two people with different opinions about the Vietnam War, such as two veterans, a military official and a reporter, or a draft resister and a parent.
2. Country Joe McDonald's "I-Feel-Like-I'm-Fixin'-to-Die Rag" has been adapted to protest everything from the oil crisis to cafeteria food. Write your own adaptation of the rag about an issue that has significance today.
3. Write an essay or editorial giving your opinion about whether violent protest is ever justified. You might use Donald Kaul's "Law and Order Chicago Style" as a model.
4. Write a poem in response to one of the people or incidents in this book.
5. Write an article or editorial about the next anniversary of the fall of Saigon.
6. Compile a list of the best literature or Web sites related to Vietnam or the 60s. Include a brief review of each source you include.
7. Write a song about whether times today are changing. You might use Bob Dylan's "The Times They Are A-Changin'" or "The Times Have Changed" as models.

Artistic Expression

1. Create a graphic or visual organizer that reflects the generation gap described in Fong-Torres' "Like a Rolling Stone."
2. Create an illustration for one of the selections in this anthology.
3. Create an editorial cartoon about changing times that could appear in your school paper.
4. Assemble images of Vietnam or the 60s (photos, paintings, brief quotations) on a Web site or in a display. Include captions that identify the image or quotation and its source and date, as well as a brief explanation of its significance.
5. Study the work of war photographers in Vietnam. Choose one image that you think deserves the award "Best Photo of the Vietnam War." Explain your choice.
6. Write a review of Maya Lin's design for the Vietnam Veterans Memorial.
7. Create a collage showing the legacy of Vietnam and the 60s.

Essay Test

Using what you have learned while reading *Times of Change: Vietnam and the 60s* and what you already know, respond to the following question. This is an open book test. Use quotations to support your response.

Prompt: What effect did the decade of the 60s have on the United States?

General Standards and Criteria for Project Evaluation

Apply those standards that fit the specific project. Some standards might not be used.

Standards	Criteria			
Areas of Assessment	*High*	*Very Good*	*Adequate*	*Needs Work*
Research and Preparation • Resources • Evidence • Deadlines • Use of Time	❏ used a variety of challenging, reliable, and appropriate resources ❏ used appropriate evidence and examples ❏ met all deadlines ❏ used any extra time to extend research	❏ used several reliable, appropriate resources ❏ made effort to use evidence and examples ❏ met deadlines ❏ used preparation time well	❏ used minimum number of resources for basic information ❏ used some evidence and examples ❏ needed encouragement to meet deadlines ❏ spent minimal time on preparation	❏ used few resources ❏ used little evidence and few examples ❏ didn't meet all deadlines ❏ spent little time on preparation
Content • Purpose • Organization • Audience Appeal • Information • Sources	❏ creatively fulfilled purpose ❏ used logical, easy-to-follow order ❏ created and maintained high audience interest ❏ covered topic with outstanding information ❏ credited sources	❏ completely fulfilled purpose ❏ used easy-to-follow order ❏ kept audience's attention ❏ covered topic with appropriate information ❏ credited sources	❏ fulfilled purpose ❏ used order that was confusing at times ❏ lost audience's attention at times ❏ covered the basics ❏ credited sources	❏ did not fulfill purpose ❏ used hard-to-follow order ❏ created little audience interest ❏ omitted important information ❏ provided incomplete credits
Visual Elements • Audience Appeal • Purpose • Effectiveness • Effort	❏ were highly interesting, easy to see and understand ❏ supported purpose ❏ communicated main ideas clearly ❏ showed outstanding effort	❏ were interesting, easy to see and understand ❏ supported purpose ❏ communicated main ideas ❏ showed effort	❏ were somewhat interesting ❏ were related to purpose ❏ generally supported main ideas ❏ showed fair effort	❏ were messy, disorganized, hard to understand ❏ were unrelated to purpose ❏ didn't support main ideas ❏ showed little effort
Written Elements • Accuracy • Revision • Details	❏ had few errors ❏ were thoroughly proofread and revised ❏ supported main ideas with rich details	❏ had few errors ❏ were proofread and revised ❏ supported main ideas	❏ had several errors ❏ needed more proofreading and revision ❏ weakly supported main ideas	❏ had many errors ❏ needed to be proofread and revised ❏ didn't support main ideas
Oral Presentation • Delivery • Props • Eye Contact	❏ spoke audibly and expressively ❏ used engaging gestures and props ❏ maintained excellent eye contact	❏ spoke audibly and expressively ❏ used gestures and props ❏ maintained good eye contact	❏ could develop more expression ❏ used few or awkward gestures and props ❏ attempted to maintain eye contact	❏ was difficult to hear ❏ used few or distracting gestures and props ❏ made little attempt to maintain eye contact

Choose from the following selections to enhance and extend the themes in this *Literature & Thought* anthology. The letters *RL* in the brackets indicate the reading level of the book listed. *IL* indicates the approximate interest level. Perfection Learning's catalog numbers are included for your ordering convenience.

Challenging

The Things They Carried by Tim O'Brien. An arc of fictional episodes, taking place in the childhoods of its characters, in the jungles of Vietnam, and back home in America two decades later. [RL 9 IL 9 +] Paperback 4221501; Cover Craft 4221502.

Average

Bloods: An Oral History of the Vietnam War by Black Veterans by Wallace Terry. Twenty black veterans of the Vietnam War discuss their war experiences in their own words. [RL 8 IL 10 +] Paperback 8878901; Cover Craft 8878902.

Born on the Fourth of July by Ron Kovic. This is Ron Kovic's story—a searing, graphic, deeply moving account of a young man whose real war began in the devastating aftermath of Vietnam. [RL 7.5 IL 10 +] Paperback 4029701; Cover Craft 4029702.

Fallen Angels by Walter Dean Myers. The critically acclaimed story of one young man's tour of duty in Vietnam and a testament to the thousands of young people who lived and died during the war. [RL 6.5 IL 7 +] Paperback 8947801; Cover Craft 8947802.

In Country by Bobbie Ann Mason. Kentucky teenager Samantha tries to find out about the war in Vietnam and about her father, who was killed there before she was born. [RL 8 IL 9 +] Paperback 4020201; Cover Craft 4020202.

The Road to Equality: American Women Since 1962 by William H. Chase. Overview of lives of American women from 1962 to 1993. Includes b&w photos, drawings, a chronology, a bibliography, and an index. Young Oxford History of Women in the United States #10. [RL 7 IL 8–12] Paperback 5481201; Cover Craft 5481202.

Shrapnel in the Heart by Laura Palmer. Heart-wrenching collection of letters left at Washington's Vietnam Veterans Memorial, and the stories of the wives, children, and friends who left them. [RL 8 IL 9 +] Paperback 8981201; Cover Craft 8981202.

Warriors Don't Cry (abridged) by Melba Pattillo Beals. An abridged young reader's edition of the vivid, gripping story of a teenager's historic battle for integration. [RL 6 IL 6 +] Paperback 4647401; Cover Craft 4647402.

The Watsons Go to Birmingham—1963 by Christopher Paul Curtis. Story narrated by Kenny, 10, about his family, the Weird Watsons of Flint, Michigan, and their trip to Birmingham, Alabama, during one of the Civil Rights Movement's most tragic events. [RL 6.1 IL 5 +] Paperback 4918201; Cover Craft 4918202.

Easy

And One for All by Theresa Nelson. Geraldine, Wing, and Sam swore eternal friendship and loyalty to one another. Now it's 1967 and Wing, a senior, thinks the Marines and Vietnam have more to offer than school, but Sam would rather march for peace. [RL 5 IL 5–9] Paperback 4216201; Cover Craft 4216202.

December Stillness by Mary Downing Hahn. Thirteen-year-old Kelly's attempts to befriend a homeless Vietnam vet end tragically, but help her come to terms with her own rocky relationship with her veteran father. [RL 4.7 IL 5–12] Paperback 4099401; Cover Craft 4099402.

Mississippi Challenge by Mildred Pitts Walter. Describes the struggle for civil rights for blacks in Mississippi from the time of slavery to the signing of the Voting Rights Act in 1965. Christopher Book Award. [RL 5.5 IL 7 +] Paperback 4960801; Cover Craft 4960802.

Park's Quest by Katherine Paterson. Eleven-year-old Park makes some startling discoveries when he travels to his grandfather's farm in Virginia to learn about his father who died in the Vietnam War. [RL 5.5 IL 5–9] Paperback 4026301; Cover Craft 4026302.

What Do You Know?

You are about to begin a unit of study on Vietnam and the 60s. Answer the following True/False questions by putting a "T" or "F" on the lines. This is not a test. Think of it as a way to find out what you already know about Vietnam and the 60s.

_____ 1. Vietnam happened too long ago to really affect my life.

_____ 2. Antiwar protesters used only peaceful tactics.

_____ 3. The draft was fair.

_____ 4. Many Americans thought that antiwar protesters and draft evaders were traitors.

_____ 5. Only people who couldn't avoid the draft served in Vietnam.

_____ 6. Woodstock gave the hippies a chance to live their dreams of a better society.

_____ 7. Young Americans influenced the government through antiwar protests.

_____ 8. Americans generally trusted what the government said about Vietnam.

_____ 9. Public pressure forced the withdrawal of American troops from Vietnam.

_____ 10. Vietnam veterans were welcomed home as heroes.

_____ 11. The memory of Vietnam makes Americans reluctant to get involved in foreign wars.

_____ 12. At the end of the Vietnam conflict, America was a different nation.

Vocabulary Test Answers

Cluster One Vocabulary Test

1. D; 2. C; 3. B; 4. A; 5. A; 6. B; 7. B; 8. D; 9. C; 10. A

Cluster Two Vocabulary Test

1. C; 2. A; 3. B; 4. A; 5. D; 6. D; 7. A; 8. B; 9. B; 10. C

Cluster Three Vocabulary Test

1. C; 2. D; 3. C; 4. B; 5. D; 6. B; 7. A; 8. D; 9. C; 10. B

Cluster Four Vocabulary Test

1. C; 2. D; 3. A; 4. D; 5. B; 6. B; 7. D; 8. B; 9. C; 10. A